THOSE BLOOMIN' SNOWDROPS!

First published in 2008 by

WOODFIELD PUBLISHING LTD
Bognor Regis ~ West Sussex ~ England ~ PO21 5EL
www.woodfieldpublishing.com

ISBN 1-84683-057-5

Those Bloomin' Snowdrops!

*A Lighthearted Look at
Life in the RAF Police*

STEPHEN R DAVIES

Woodfield

Woodfield Publishing Ltd

Bognor Regis ~ West Sussex ~ PO21 5EL
telephone 01243 821234 ~ **e-mail** enquiries@woodfieldpublishing.co.uk

Interesting and informative books on a variety of subjects

For full details of all our published titles, visit our website at
www.woodfieldpublishing.co.uk

ODE TO THE RAF POLICE

You see them all over the camp at night
Uniformed zombies in hats of white
They're seeking here, they're seeking there
So all you baddies best beware

A drunken Rock[1] can make their night
He'll probably give up without a fight
They'll lock him in a lonely cell
And tell you that he fought like hell

The ones in suits are the SIB
With cases to crack and places to be
They travel the country in nice fast cars
To put those villains behind prison bars

The CI men are the secret group
Trying to break the spying loop
Security is their full-time role
Working away like moles in a hole

The ones with dogs are a different breed
They keep their beasties on the lead
On the word of command they're ready to bite
Only a fool would take on such a fight

You see them all over the camp at night
Uniformed zombies in hats of white
With blues lights flashing in the dark
They're really out to make their mark.....

---

[1] A member of the RAF Regiment (known by the rest of the RAF as Rock Apes.

~ CONTENTS ~

The Author ~ drawn by Janner Pascoe.

The Author

Stephen R Davies has a wicked sense of humour and was a member of the RAF Police for 25 years. In 1975 he joined the RAF as a policeman and during his service completed tours of duty in the UK and numerous other countries around the globe. He qualified as a specialist in RAF Police special investigation and counter-intelligence matters and successfully completed the Home Office detective training program and drug enforcement courses with the UK civil police, the Royal Navy and the United States Air Force Office of Special Investigations. In 1991 he qualified as an instructor and lectured at the Airmans' Command School and the RAF Police School. The highpoint of his career was a four-month exchange to New Zealand.

In the spring of 2000, he retired from the RAF and together with his wife, moved out to Portugal where they now live. The author's research into the RAF Police continues and he is currently working to record the first 100 years (1918 – 2018) of this unique branch of the RAF.

Other books by the author include:

Fiat Justitia published in April 1997 by Minerva Press.

RAF Police Dogs on Patrol published in November 2005 by Woodfield Publishing Limited.

RAF Police Operations in Europe 1918 – 2005 published in September 2006 by Woodfield Publishing Limited.

RAF Police: Cape Town to Kabul published in November 2007 by Woodfield Publishing Limited.

RAF Police: Bombay to Ascension published in September 2008 by Woodfield Publishing Limited.

Acknowledgements

I would like to express my sincere thanks to the many serving and former serving members of the RAF Police who have contributed towards this book. Indeed, for many, it was the first time that they have made a formal confession of their past activities, but all, it has to be said, in a very worthy cause. Sadly, a number of the individual artists who drew the cartoons from the 1950s are no longer with us but by including their work in this book at least their names and their work will hopefully live on. Again, I have included a number of stories and cartoons within the book, even though I have no idea as to the identity of the authors. I hope that if any claimant recognises their work, that they will support this initiative and contact me. Finally, I would like to express my thanks to Derek Knight-Messenger over in Canada, who in addition to providing me with a number of his own cartoons, very kindly agreed to design the cover of the book.

Stephen R Davies
Obidos Portugal 2008

MY FIRST ARREST

Derek Knight-Messenger

At the tender age of 18, I began my service with the RAF Police in the autumn of 1952 and was posted to RAF Cardington near Bedford. After my arrival interview with Sergeant Hawley, a congenial giant, who was the senior NCO in charge of the Main Guardroom, it was decided that I should commence my duties on the night shift; apparently it would help me to settle into my new career as it was usually quiet, with little happening between 2359 and 0800 hours. The guardroom staff comprised; Sergeant Hawley; his deputy and NCO in charge of investigations, Corporal Moffat; and 8 corporals who worked in pairs to cover the three eight hour shifts.

I was guided through my first night shift by my mentor Corporal Abe Walmsley who was in charge of the shift. He was an affable person, and obviously a very capable and efficient policeman. There were half a dozen large cells within the guardroom that were almost always in use with as many as five detainees in each cell. Strangely, the regulations dictated that each cell could only have an odd number of occupants; 1, 3 or 5 men, never 2, 4 or 6. In addition to controlling entry and exit via the main gate, I was also responsible for making the early morning rounds to wake up the cooks and other permanent staff detailed for early shifts. We also had two dog handlers who came on duty at 2359 hours to conduct random patrols of the station.

In the small hours, Corporal Walmsley received several telephone calls from nervous wives living in the married quarters at Shortstown Estates who reported hearing and seeing two male prowlers attempting to enter their homes. Soon after, others were calling to say that their homes had actually been broken into and items had been stolen. Unfortunately, in the days before personal radios were standard issue, we had no way of contacting our dog handlers until they telephoned in at an agreed time. The married quarters were located off the actual station, some distance from the guardroom and as we had no available means of transport, I was ordered by Corporal Walmsley to make my way there to investigate the situation.

It was a clear bright, moonlit night and the weather was mild when I duly set off on foot through the main gate and down the road to the estates. I was dressed in my No 2 Home Dress uniform with lead-weighted trouser bottoms tucked into my gaiters, and my heavy *bulled-up* size 12 hob-nailed boots were crunching on the gravel as I made my way. I was armed only with a police whistle, my pencil and police note-book; I had no truncheon or handcuffs as they could only be issued on the authority of a commissioned officer.

It took 20 minutes of fast walking to arrive there during which time I recalled instructions taught during my basic training;

> 'When a policeman proceeds to the scene, except in exceptional circumstances, he will walk, not run! He must not arrive out of breath.'

Initially, I marched importantly around the streets and although I was startled by the occasional cat gliding about like a shadow, there was no sign of the prowlers. Perhaps, I thought to myself, the intruders had got all they could carry and had already left the area. However, on impulse, I decided to crouch down and hide behind some bushes at the entrance to the estate; perhaps the prowlers had hidden from my view as they spotted the sparkling brass on my gleaming white blancoed webbing or perhaps they had heard my boots crashing onto the pavements.

As luck had it, within minutes along came two slightly built, middle-aged men carrying between them a large bag; obviously stuffed with something heavy. I waited until they had passed my hiding place then I pounced. I quickly came up behind them, grabbing them both by their outside wrists.

Within seconds I had their arms pinned high up and no doubt painfully behind their backs. Much to my surprise neither struggled nor tried to resist arrest but instead, they pleaded for mercy in pitiful tones and assured me that I didn't need to treat them so roughly.

One of them even added, *"It's a fair cop governor!"*

Both readily admitted that they had broken into several houses and that the loot was in the sack which they were holding with their inside free hands. By then, a number of residents had heard the commotion and had come out of their homes to see just was going on. Frankly, I felt somewhat nervous when I realized that I had a long walk back to the guardroom with my two prisoners and their loot but with no assistance. I wasn't quite ready to take the word of two confessed burglars who promised to cooperate but apart from whimpering pitifully all the way back to the guardroom, they caused me no problems.

The game is afoot!

drawn by Derek Knight-Messenger

Awaiting our arrival at the guardroom with Corporal Walmsley were the orderly officer, a short, baby-faced, excited young pilot officer; the orderly corporal; the local bobby and former RAF Policeman, Constable Brian Contance; and two detectives from the Bedfordshire Police. I explained what had happened and expressed my surprise that the two men had not put up any resistance.

Constable Contance however, explained that both men were well-known to the local police and had in fact just been released from prison the previous morning. Both were professional burglars with a long list of previous convictions but had no history of violence. In fact, Constable Contance assured me that they were both only too glad to be heading back to prison where they would rejoin their old mates and where they would once more be sure of a warm place to sleep which provided three square meals each day.

Somehow, I didn't feel quite such a *hero* anymore but more like a *persecutor* who had frog-marched two pitiful old jailbirds some distance up the road to the guardroom.

The detectives searched them and read them their rights, addressing both by their first names, rather like old friends. Then they drove off into the night towards Bedford.

When all was quiet again, we started to hear the early morning birds chirping merrily and Corporal Walmsley turned to me with a cheerful smile and said:

"Well Derek me lad, that's your first shift almost over. The dog handlers will soon be here reporting in for their tea. Be a good chap and put the kettle on will you!"

ON THE JOB TRAINING

Stephen R Davies

A new arrival joined the night shift. Although he was eighteen and had passed his training without any major problems, his boyish face and rosy red cheeks made him look more like a cherub from a church painting rather than the stereotype RAF Policeman. However, he was now part of the team and after a quick briefing he was assigned to join one of the more experienced men so that he could settle in to the routine and learn the practicalities of the job.

It was just after midnight and as I was passing the control room I noticed that the fire door was open and several of the guys were standing there looking onto the airfield laughing at something. At that time the airfield was closed and all flying had stopped for the night however, I was curious to know what was going on, so I approached, and someone handed me the powerful set of binoculars that we kept in the control room.

Following their directions I focused onto a strange convoy that was moving up the main runway, which comprised of two RAF Police Land-Rovers, side by side, complete with flashing blue lights. However, as I homed in on the scene I could see illuminated in the headlights of the vehicles our new *cherub* who seemed to be brushing the runway furiously with a rather large broom. Clipped to his right shoulder was a red light and clipped to his left shoulder was a green light.

When I asked the guys what he was doing they replied that they were showing him how to carry out a *security sweep* of the airfield!

It was almost as good as the one where another new RAF Police arrival was told to report to the end of the runway and turn on the large taps to flood the airfield because the duty Air Traffic controller had advised them that a seaplane was about to land.

You be doin' the Salvage Dump, 'Erbert, while I nip along to the W.R.A.F. Site

Drawn by Flight Sergeant 'Shep' Shepherdson

RE-CYCLED TAKE-AWAY

Stewart McArdle

Sometime in the early 1970s I was a dog handler stationed at RAF Machrihanish on the west coast of Scotland. I recall that there were a couple of *frightfully posh* assistant air traffic controllers stationed on the unit who obviously thought that they were something rather special and far superior to us mere dog handlers. Anyway, one day in the Airmen's Mess *Mr and Mrs Posh,* as they were known, made the mistake of making an adverse comment about dog handlers during a conversation and although they were not aware, I overheard it and thought that it was about time that they were taken down a peg or two.

The following day after acquiring a rubber hot water bottle into which I had poured a can of chunky vegetable soup, I entered the mess with four other dog handlers and we quickly found a clean table next to the couple and started a loud conversation about the amount of beer we had drunk the night before that had been followed by a huge Chinese take-away.

I had the hot water bottle down the front of my shirt so when we had their full attention and started getting the usual looks of disgust, I started to make out that I was about to vomit and as I bent forward I squeezed the bottle and sprayed the vegetable soup all over the table.

The look of revulsion on the faces of *Mr and Mrs Posh* was truly a picture but before they could react the other dog handlers quickly grabbed their spoons and started to scoop up the soup making comments like: *'We can't waste a good Chinese take-away, it probably tastes better the second time around'.*

As they gobbled up the mess in front of them, *Mr and Mrs Posh* made a very hasty retreat looking rather green around the gills and for some strange reason they never sat near the dog handlers again.

"Not on there you clot"

drawn by Flight Sergeant 'Shep' Shepherdson

THE RECRUITING DRIVE

John Law

It was the mid 1970s and three rather mean-looking RAF Police investigators; Frank Merrick, Jeff Davies and John Law, had just finished giving evidence at a pre-court martial hearing at RAF Valley in North Wales. Because there was nothing much happening elsewhere they decided to return to their headquarters in Northolt on the western edge of London via the longer but more scenic route through Wales and then across country towards the capital.

That night, the three weary travellers came upon a tavern in the middle of nowhere close to the Brecon Beacons and decided to book in for the night. The landlord was most hospitable and the bar was decorated with old weapons which the three investigators took a great deal of interest in, much to the curiosity of the locals.

After a while, a couple of the locals could not contain their inquisitiveness any longer and wanted to know who the three strangers were. At that point, it was John Law who spoke up and said,

"Well, you had better ask the Colonel that," indicating over to Frank Merrick.

Immediately one of the brighter sparks in the group responded with, "I know, you're mercenaries looking for recruits." (*At that time there had been lots of newspaper reports on the activities of foreign mercenaries operating in African conflicts*).

Of course, the three investigators, who by then were being treated like VIPs, continued to lead the locals on and that night as the beer flowed and the pub became packed with potential recruits, all wanting to sign up to go off to fight in exotic places.

"May I see your 1250 please?"

Artist unknown

FITNESS TEST FAILURES

Stephen R Davies

Corporal Adrian Palmer arrived at RAF Wyton during the baking hot summer of 1976 together with his police dog, Air dog Mick. Both were new to the service, Mick was a recently acquired gift dog, and Adrian had just completed his basic police course and the training to become a dog handler.

After being at Wyton for only a few days, Adrian decided to exercise his dog and at the same time explore the local area around the base. It was a particularly hot day when they left the dog section mid morning, intending to find their way down to a path by the nearby river that would take them through some pretty villages towards Huntingdon.

As the hours passed and the temperatures continued to soar, a number of Adrian's colleagues began to get worried that he and his dog may have got lost or that something worse had happened. It was pretty hot out there and he had not taken any water with him on the walk. Although Mick possessed a good temperament, technically, Adrian should not have taken him beyond the bounds of the RAF base.

Another hour passed and the search party sent out to look for them returned with no news. At that point it was decided that if they had not reappeared in another fifteen minutes then the boss would have to be told and a full search mounted to find them.

With literally minutes to spare, a taxi approached the main gate to the base and there in the front passenger seat was Adrian, well in fact, it could have been anybody really, because Air dog Mick, a huge beast, was sitting on his lap looking out towards us.

As the pair baled out of the vehicle and Adrian paid the fare, we gathered around to find out what had happened.

It seemed that they had gone much further than expected and when he and his dog, found themselves too tired to walk back, Adrian hailed a taxi and after showing the driver his warrant card, persuaded a somewhat confused driver to take them back to Wyton. After that, Adrian didn't take his dog for another walk beyond the boundary of the base.

"Hopkins, there is a suggestion that your dog may be lacking in moral fibre!"

drawn by 'Roberts'

SQUADRON EMBLEMS

Gerald White

Almost all RAF flying squadrons have a badge and motto. The badges, approved by the Royal College of Heraldry, usually follow a standard pattern with the centre piece and motto being the only difference from badge to badge as these examples from No 27 Squadron, No 83 Squadron and No 617 (*The Dambusters*) Squadron will testify.

Of course, No 617 (*The Dambusters*) Squadron, under the command of Wing Commander Guy Gibson VC, was famous for breaching German dams with the bouncing bombs during World War II. As with all arms of the British Armed Forces, RAF squadrons are immensely proud of their historic background but sometimes their enthusiasm borders on the eccentric.

In 1968, the three squadrons mentioned above were stationed at RAF Scampton in Lincolnshire and were always trying to outdo each other for the top place.

During the summer of that year, the Station Commander; Group Captain McKay, paid a visit to the RAF Police manning the Airfield Security Control Centre. As he was being briefed by Sergeant J Schembri and Corporal G White, the 27 Squadron aircrew coach drove past the building with a huge brightly painted model of an elephant (*similar to that in its badge*) fixed to the roof.

Noting the strange looks that the police were giving the vehicle, which was probably breaking a number of road traffic regulations, the Group Captain quickly commented,

"Ah well, the boys have got to have their spot of fun I suppose."

He then went on to say that 83 Squadron had also brightened up their coach by fixing a stag's head with an eight pronged antler (*similar to that in its badge*) to the bonnet.

He then went on to say that 617 Squadron's commanding officer was however, at a complete loss to compete with the latest craze. He had apparently become even more frustrated when his two contemporaries had suggested that in keeping with his squadron's badge, he could always kick the radiator of his coach in and allow the water to gush out.

For a split second, there was silence, and then everyone present burst out laughing as the penny dropped.

AIRMAN!!!

drawn by Flight Sergeant 'Shep' Shepherdson

A PAIN IN THE BUTT

Steve Burton

Towards the end of 1983, I was stationed on Ascension Island, located far from everywhere in the middle of the South Atlantic. Employed on shift work, I was usually teamed up with Corporal Derek Marjoram and I recall a rather amusing incident which occurred on Christmas Eve.

While I remained in the police office at *Wideawake airhead* that evening, Derek took the Land Rover and went out to carry out a patrol of the island, which only covered seven or eight square miles. After a couple of hours Derek came across an unfortunate soul who appeared, on the face of it, to be very inebriated, somewhat confused and wandering around in the *bondu* near the Officers Mess at the recently-opened RAF base at Travellers Hill.

When Derek approached, he realised that the airman was, in fact, the RAF Base Commander's driver and he had definitely had a few too many. However, not wishing to spoil the driver's Christmas, Derek tried to establish where he was going, so that he could ensure that he got there safely.

At the best of times drunks are not the best people to reason with and this one was certainly no different. Taking great exception to being stopped by the police, the airman subjected Derek to a torrent of foul and abusive language, so Derek arrested him and led him back to the Land Rover, intending to take him to the police station cells in Georgetown for the night.

Placing his prisoner into the vehicle proved quite difficult, however, because every time Derek sat him down on the seat, the airman leapt up and became quite agitated, issuing more verbal abuse.

After a while Derek got quite frustrated and radioed for me to attend his location to assist. That, of course, proved difficult, because Derek was in the only RAF Police vehicle and I was a good few miles from where he needed assistance. Anyway, while I was trying to get additional transport, Derek had managed to calm the airman down and had established the source of the problem, which was somewhat unusual.

A short time later, Derek telephoned me again in the police office and explained that he was now at the Georgetown Hospital awaiting the arrival of the doctor and not at the Georgetown police station as had first been intended. Derek, went on to explain that his prisoner had been a *right pain in the butt* and just when I was expecting to hear that the situation had turned nasty for Derek he went on to tell me that the drunken airman had left the Officers Mess kitchen intending to return to his accommodation and had taken a shortcut across the *bondu*.[2]

On his way, he apparently 'got caught short' and in order to relieve his discomfort, had dropped his trousers, squatted down and promptly fell backwards into a prickly pear thicket. As a result, his buttocks took delivery of between 40-60 prickly pear spikes. So, unbeknown to Derek at the time, when he was forcing his prisoner to sit down in the vehicle, the painful spikes were being forced deeper into the airman's buttocks.

Perhaps it was the pain that finally brought the airman to his senses when he explained to Derek what had happened.

Although the spikes were successfully removed in the hospital it was several days before the airman could sit down properly again...

---

[2] *Bondu* – rough volcanic terrain on Ascension where a considerable amount of prickly pear thickets grow in abundance.

A MATTER OF INTERPRETATION

Gerald White

On one occasion in 1964, Corporal Gerald White was on duty in the guardroom one evening when the duty clerk requested that the Orderly Officer be called out to authorise (by signature) a signal to be sent off the station. The Orderly Officer was duly informed but because it was raining requested that the RAF Police collect him in their vehicle from the Officers Mess.

Shortly after, Corporal White drove up to the Officers Mess and the Orderly Officer, who was a young pink-faced Pilot Officer, got into the mini and, no doubt annoyed at being called out, asked to be taken to the Station Headquarters to meet the duty Clerk.

At that point, Corporal White noticed that the officer was wearing his duty armband upside down and so brought the matter to the officer's attention.

The cocky young officer however replied,

"For goodness sake Corporal how on earth can an armband, which has the letters 'OO' on it, be upside down?"

To which Corporal White simply replied,

"But Sir, the full stops are at the top."

In the mid 1960s the Station Warrant Officer (SWO) at RAF Dishforth in Yorkshire was a highly decorated wartime Polish fighter pilot and although his piloting skills were undoubted, he did have a certain amount of difficulty in mastering the English language.

Part of his job each week was to prepare the Station Routine Orders for publication and on one such occasion an order was published regarding the domestic tasks to be carried out by the airmen and airwomen during a forthcoming domestic evening. The order duly informed;

'Wednesday 5th June will be a domestic evening, airmen living in Billets will wash the windows, as well as the Airwomen'.

On another occasion, the SWO was overheard detailing a working party of airmen in the transit block to: 'dismantle the beds from room one and remantle them in room four.'

As he left the room there was a certain amount of laughter from the working party and a stunned silence as he quickly returned and said, "Did I say something funny?"

Artist unknown

BEWARE OF THE SQUIRRELS

Author Unknown

During ground defence training at a RAF Base in Lincolnshire, a RAF Police corporal disguised as a tree trunk made a sudden move that was spotted by the unit's RAF Regiment officer.

"You simpleton!" the officer barked. "Don't you know that by jumping and yelling in that way you could have endangered the lives of your entire section?"

"Yes sir," the corporal answered apologetically. "But, if I may say in my defence, that I did stand still when a flock of pigeons used me for target practice, and I never moved a muscle when a large dog urinated on my lower branches, but when two squirrels ran up my trouser leg and I heard the bigger one say, Let's eat one now and save the other until winter – that did it!"

I think the last promotion has somewhat disillusioned our Harry . . .

drawn by 'Milne'

R·A·F TYPES

ON DUTY

Station Warrant Officer

OFF DUTY

drawn by Flight Sergeant 'Shep' Shepherdson

Shep

---

20 ~ *Those Bloomin' Snowdrops!*

TRUE MASTERPIECES

Stewart McArdle

In 1976 Corporal Stewart McArdle, who was in charge of the Dog Section at RAF Woodhall Spa, received a telephone call from the boss one morning asking if he would put on a dog demonstration for a group of newly commissioned officers from the RAF College at Cranwell. As always, Stewart quickly agreed to show off the skill of his handlers and their dogs.

When Stewart had first taken over the Dog Section some time before, there had been a collection of old aircraft photographs mounted on hardboard all around the walls of the crew room. However, they were boring and the images had faded and did little to cheer the place up.

To rectify the situation and brighten up the rest room, Stewart had the photographs taken down and, having discovered a colourful surplus of paint in the storeroom, set about pouring the contents of each can over the hardboard backing of the photographs.

After a few days of drying, Stewart was pleased to find that he had a pretty impressive set of highly colourful psychedelic paintings which when hung back on the walls definitely helped to brighten the room up.

Anyway, on the day of the visit, the group of young RAF officers, 'straight out of their box', were having coffee in the rest room while the handlers were preparing for the demonstration. Some of the officers were standing, hands behind their backs, discussing the merits of the fine abstract artwork on the walls and what the artist might have been thinking about when he painted them.

Stewart, who couldn't help overhearing, was trying hard not to snigger.

The officers then began talking, rather seriously, about what they each saw in the pictures; one for instance saw a pirate with his ship, while others saw a block of flats or a scene from a riverbank.

Stewart's boss, who knew full well who had created the masterpieces, was standing with the group when he suddenly announced,

"Corporal McArdle, these officers are very interested in the artist who created these rather fine paintings," and with a wink continued, "Can you please enlighten these gentlemen?"

"Yes Sir, replied Stewart. "Gentlemen, I am the artist and my method was simply to *splash surplus paint all over them...*"

Stewart then went on to explain his method of painting in more detail, just as the group of officers, clearly embarrassed, announced,

"Well of course, we knew that all along, we were just having you on corp."

"Yes Sir, of course you were!"

drawn by 'CHR'

THE CAMEL TRAIN

Barrie Dove

In 1959 Barrie Dove was a RAF Police dog handler serving out in Aden at RAF Khormaksar. He recalls that during his tour the Arab Bedouins used to organise an annual 'camel train' through Aden carrying huge quantities of 'Qat'; an organic substance that provided effects very similar to those obtained from Marijuana.

The camel train travelled at night and each camel driver had several camels tethered together with the last displaying a red lantern to the rear. As the camels followed the one in front, the lead camel driver remained awake 'steering' the train while his fellow drivers travelling behind slept on their beasts as they travelled.

The camel train left Sheik Othman and made its way through Steamer Point and Crater passing close to RAF Khormaksar and that is where the dog handlers waited for them. As the camel train approached, a couple of the dog handlers would very quietly approach the last group of camels and after ensuring that the owner was asleep they would carefully turn the lead camel around.

It was usually dawn when the confused camel driver woke up only to realise that he was back in Sheik Othman.

Just another example of disrupting the transportation of dangerous substances I suppose!

Drawn by 'Milne'

A VISIT BY THE A-O-C

Stephen R Davies

The Air-Officer-Commanding (AOC) was coming to carry out his annual formal inspection of RAF Wyton, and as always a big panic was created well in advance; anything that stood still was polished, painted or swept. On the plus side however, there was always the chance that the broken window might be replaced, the leaky tap repaired or that the barrack accommodation might even receive a new lick of paint. In the weeks preceding the visit several rehearsals were held during which RAF Police NCOs were placed at strategic road junctions to control traffic and ensure priority for the VIP motorcade at all costs!

At the final briefing it was emphasized by the new station commander that nothing at all was to go wrong; after all, the most critically tuned brains on the unit had planned everything down to the finest detail in order to impress, so what could possibly go wrong? The ground crew on the squadron lines had been scrubbed up and issued with dazzling white overalls; the aircraft, all lined up on the dispersal areas, gleamed in the sunshine; the kerbstones had all received a fresh lick of white paint, and the RAF Police in their best ceremonial uniforms, white hats, white belts and white gloves looked smarter that any Regiment of Guards on parade.

All RAF Police NCOs were dispatched to their assigned posts around the unit one hour before the AOC was due to arrive. The RAF Police vehicle had been polished to a high lustre and young Davies, recently out of training, joined up with a senior corporal; Mick Gregory, to provide the lead escort in the VIP motorcade during its tour of the unit. Bang on time, the AOC's helicopter landed and the motorcade comprising the police vehicle, the AOC's staff car, the station commander's staff car and a host of camp followers moved into position. After reviewing the guard of honour the AOC stepped into his car and the motorcade moved off to its first port of call; one of the aircraft squadrons. Suddenly, as the police vehicle continued along the pre-arranged route, the AOC's car and the rest of the motorcade turned off to the left towards the domestic site...

The domestic site?

Gregory and Davies were aghast to have lost the AOC even before their first stop; nobody had told them of any change in the itinerary.

Quickly, Davies used the radio to alert the control room and Gregory spun the car around in hot pursuit. They arrived at the Sergeant's Mess just as the AOC leapt from his car and entered the front door to surprise those inside, who were not expecting him to descend upon them.

While the AOC was well aware of the official itinerary, he had decided to inspect the places which were not listed, just to see if things had been prepared to his satisfaction.

In the meantime, out on the squadron lines, concerned air-crew, ground crew and assorted personnel were looking at their watches and rechecking their copy of the itinerary...

'nothing could possibly go wrong...

everything had been planned down to the smallest detail...

the phone lines started to buzz...

After causing just a slight amount of panic within the Sergeant's Mess, the AOC's motorcade moved off again, with Davies and Gregory paying particular attention as to its next possible port of call.

Again, within a few minutes, the motorcade veered off and the two policemen were forced into taking a short cut around different buildings to the next place that the AOC wanted to surprise.

During the hours that followed, while Gregory and Davies attempted to predict the AOC's intentions, he, with ceremonial sword dangling from his uniform, pursued by his *aide-de-camp*, continued to descend upon the sections excluded from his official itinerary, causing all manner of mayhem as he tested contingency plans by setting off fire alarms or invoking various *disasters*.

Later that afternoon, after complimenting the new station commander on a job well done, the AOC returned to the airfield to re-board his helicopter.

After saying goodbye to the station commander, he looked across to the police vehicle and indicated for the policemen to approach.

In his haste to get out of the car however, Davies ended up splitting his trousers wide open at the crotch, an event which didn't go unnoticed by the AOC, who smiled and expressed his genuine thanks to the two men for coping splendidly throughout the day with all the confusion he had caused.

Confusion it may have been, but boring it certainly was not!

"They've got to walk around in two's—one can read, the other can write—it would be a 50% saving in manpower if we ever get snoops that do both!"

Drawn by Flight Sergeant 'Shep' Shepherdson

"Sergeant, there's an hofficer wot's 'ere to inspect your big balloons."

Drawn by Derek Knight-Messenger

LOW-FLY ZONE

Gordon Smith

In 1958 Corporal Smith and Air dog Ranee had just started their shift one evening at RAF Aldergrove and were walking around the perimeter track, heading for their patrol area, when a Shackleton aircraft came into land, touched down, and quickly took off again, roaring over the startled dog handler and his dog.

"Gee..." thought Corporal Smith, "That was exciting!"

He naturally assumed that the aircraft was practicing *circuits and bumps* (landing and taking-off again).

However, at the end of his shift, Corporal Smith was ordered to report to the Orderly Officer, who gave him a right dressing down for apparently ignoring the red light, which in turn caused the Shackleton to abort its landing.

Unfortunately, no-one had ever told Corporal Smith about red lights on the airfield ~ and he hadn't actually *seen* a red light anyway...

He did however, enjoy the air show!

drawn by 'Angel'

ALMOST 'OUT FOR A DUCK'

Brian Taylor

In May 1950, Corporal Brian Taylor was stationed with the RAF Police Section at RAF St Hubertus near Lubeck in North West Germany awaiting his demob from the service.

About half a mile away from the unit, across open country, a river divided East and West Germany. At the time, members of the RAF Police were routinely issued with .38 Smith & Wesson revolvers and six rounds of ammunition each. A dog handler; Corporal Jock Ross, had acquired a further twenty rounds of ammunition from somewhere, without having to sign for them.

After some discussion, Corporal's Taylor, Ross and another dog handler called Don thought it would be a good idea to organise a duck hunt on their next day off. The extra rounds of ammunition were safely hidden away and recovered a few days later for the duck hunt in the area close to the aforementioned river.

Corporal Ross took along his dog, which he thought would be ideal to flush out the ducks from the reed beds along the riverbank and, after selecting an area they thought was just right, the dog was sent in and soon after a great many ducks took to the air in panic. As they did so, Corporal Taylor took aim with his revolver and continued firing until he was out of ammunition.

Unfortunately, and not surprisingly, he failed to bring down a single duck. However, at that point, a noise on the other side of the river caught their attention and within a few minutes about thirty or so heavily armed Russian border guards were pointing their rifles towards them.

The shoot was hastily abandoned and the three NCOs and their dog followed the example of the ducks and took flight into the cover of the reeds.

Although the excitement across the river continued for some time, thankfully no-one opened fire and the three *duck hunters* were able to make their way back to their unit.

Although in the safety of the barrack room they were able to laugh the matter off, their hunting adventure could quite easily have started off a rather nasty cross-border incident with them becoming the hunted instead of the hunters.

Drawn by Tony Paley

A COSTLY ENCOUNTER

Alfred Bernstone

It was Christmas Eve 1965 and I was the duty investigator on call at the Headquarters Provost & Security Services stationed in Singapore. I was sound asleep in the bed provided within the Provost Section when my slumbers were rudely shattered by a young RAF Police corporal who was working the night shift.

As I came too, he informed me that an airman wanted to report a crime and handed me the telephone.

The call was from a rather irate airman who complained that he and his mate had paid two prostitutes $50 each only to find that when they arrived at their room the two ladies of the night were transvestites.

Somewhat shocked by their discovery, the airmen had demanded their money back, but the transvestites, known locally as *Catamites*, refused to hand back the cash.

When I asked the airman where he and his mate were, they answered 'Deskah Road.'

At that point I told him that they were in an 'Out of Bounds' area and as such, had two choices;

one – for me to go to them and arrest them both for being 'out of bounds', or

two – to put the incident down to experience and forget it.

The airman abruptly rang off, I returned to my slumbers and heard nothing more of the matter.

GOODMAN

"If it wasn't for blokes like me, you lot would be out of a job . . "

Drawn by 'Goodman'

BOMBER COMMAND CALLING...

John Matthews

RAF Beaulieu was situated on the edge of the New Forest and operated to guard the contents of three or four large hangers, although we were never told what they contained; it may have been the remains of a flying saucer for all we knew!

This cornerstone of the *Cold War* consisted of a flight lieutenant (who was the CO) and his batman, one cook, one clerk, one admin sergeant, one fireman with a Land Rover, Acme fire extinguisher and a bucket of sand, and nine RAF Policemen under the control of a substantive corporal.

This backwater sleepy-hollow had an airfield with one long concrete runway and a perimeter track, both littered with cracks from which a profusion of wild flowers bloomed (none of which were snowdrops, incidentally).

It was a very quiet Saturday afternoon and I was alone on duty in the guardroom when the telephone rang.

The following conversation took place:

"Good afternoon, guardroom RAF Beaulieu, LAC Matthews speaking."

"Good afternoon, this is LACW Smith from Bomber Command Operations. What are your weather conditions?"

"Not bad for September, thank you."

"What do you mean, 'not bad for September' – what's your current visibility?"

"North East to North West about 5 miles, all other directions vary between 50 and 200 yards."

"What sort of an answer is that?"

"Well I can see for miles over the airfield and over an expanse of gorse, but the other directions are obscured by all the trees of the New Forest."

"Put me through to your CO ... please." (presumably realising that she might be talking to the RAF Police).

"Sorry, he's not here right now."

"Well then, put the senior duty officer on the line."

"I'm sorry, but we don't have one."

"Please hold on..."

Well-spoken male voice: "Good afternoon, this is Squadron Leader Compton-Jones. To whom am I speaking?"

"LAC Matthews, 4166880, Royal Air Force Police, Sir."

"You are upsetting my secretary, please put me through to whoever is in charge."

"Actually Sir, I'm in charge this afternoon."

"Look, we have an aircraft with one engine on fire which needs to land very soon, can you mobilise your fire and crash teams?"

I quickly explained about the CO, the sergeant and the senior police corporal all being away for the weekend, while most of the others had gone off shopping in Lymington, leaving me, and the only fireman (with his bucket of sand, etc), whom I outranked by a couple of weeks, in control of the camp.

A few splutters and a curse came from the other end of the line and then it went dead.

At the tender age of 18, this, I thought, was the end of my promising RAF career ... with only 7 months service in.

Later that afternoon the telephone rang once again and the following conversation took place.

"Good afternoon, RAF Beaulieu ..."

"Is that LAC Matthews?"

"Yes Sir."

"Hello again, this is Squadron Leader Compton-Jones from Bomber Command Operations. I thought you'd like to know that our aircraft landed safely 30 minutes ago at Burtonwood. Sorry to have caused you any problems, but you came up first alphabetically in our list of operational airfields... I will see that it is deleted... Goodbye."

'What a nice officer,' I thought and, looking back, I never did meet a nasty one.

When the other chaps came back from town they thought I had made it all up ~ and denied any suggestion of a *leg-pull* on their part, which I had suspected at the start.

CATCH US IF YOU CAN

Clive Titcomb

Clive Titcomb and Jim Henry were RAF Police dog handlers at RAF Akrotiri in Cyprus during the 1960s. At the time the officer responsible for the dog section was Flying Officer Andrew Seymour, who later became Provost Marshal.

In order to ensure that his men were alert and carrying out their patrols of the airfield properly, he used to pay them frequent unannounced visits during the hours of darkness.

The dog handlers, of course, had a system in place to warn each other when he was out and about, so whenever he visited, he always found the dog handlers alert and patrolling their assigned areas in a most efficient manner and never caught anyone doing anything they shouldn't have been doing, which at times he thought was odd...

One evening, close to Christmas, Clive and Jim were on one of the aircraft dispersal areas listening to the British Forces Broadcasting Service when the announcer asked listeners to phone in with their music requests and Christmas greetings.

Clive, in his wisdom, phoned up and asked for a record to be played for Flying Officer Seymour from all the dog handlers at RAF Akrotiri, but asked that he should remain anonymous.

Some time later, the request for Flying Officer Seymour from all the dog handlers at RAF Akrotiri was played.

It was 'Catch Us If You Can' by the Dave Clarke Five.

Jim and Clive thought it was a great tribute until, at the end of the song, the announcer said: "...and that was from Corporal Clive Titcomb and all the RAF Police dog handlers at RAF Akrotiri."

Most people on the base heard the request, including Flying Officer Seymour, who was in the Officers' Mess.

The next day Corporal Titcomb was duly reprimanded by his boss ~ but it had been well worth it!

Drawn by Derek Knight-Messenger

COMMUNICATION BREAKDOWN

Stephen R Davies

In the office of the criminal investigators working for the Southern Region Headquarters, my desk was up against one wall next to that of a colleague's and together we shared a single telephone. On one particular day, everyone working in the office was notified that the telephones cables of a unit within our area; RAF Brize Norton, had been severed during construction work, and as a result, it would be impossible to telephone anyone on the unit for several hours until repairs were carried out.

Unfortunately, for some reason, my colleague Moss was out of the office when the news came in.

Some time later, Moss returned to his desk in a rather foul mood, snatched up the telephone and dialled a number. After several attempts it was clear that he was having problems getting a connection and his mood was becoming even darker.

He continued in his attempts and during his angry mutterings I and some of the others in the office realised that he was trying to get through to someone at Brize Norton.

As if by an invisible conspiracy no-one in the office said a thing but merely sat back to watch Moss's frustration become more intense.

After several more unsuccessful attempts and several curses he slammed the telephone down and stormed over to the filing cabinet to retrieve a file.

At that point, I picked up the receiver and dialled the police office at RAF Lyneham and spoke to the unit investigator about a case we were working on. My conversation, however, was briefly interrupted by Moss from the other side of the office, telling me to hurry up as he had an urgent call to make.

Having finished my conversation anyway, I said quite plainly into the receiver, "Okay, I'll be over to Brize Norton tomorrow morning so I'll see you then".

At that point, just as the telephone receiver was being lowered towards its cradle, everyone in the office was treated to a rather panic-stricken Moss leaping across the room in his attempt to grab it before the connection to Brize Norton was severed.

Frustratingly, he didn't quite make it!

As he snatched the phone in a frenzy, I merely said,

"I'm sorry Moss, did you want Brize Norton?"

His response was quite unrepeatable.

For the following half hour or so, he continued, quite unsuccessfully, to dial Brize Norton, until we put him out of his misery by letting him in on the secret.

" GUESS WOT - ME AND YOUR DAUGHTER IS GONNA BE MARRIED, DADDY!"

Drawn by Derek Knight-Messenger

ALL IN THE FINGER ACTION

Steve Burchell

On RAF stations where the police were routinely armed with pistols and machine guns, a rigid system of loading and unloading the weapons was closely supervised by the shift sergeant.

At the end of the shift, after the magazine containing the ammunition had been removed from the weapon and the weapon itself had been inspected by the sergeant to ensure that it was free of ammunition, the police NCO would be required to unload the bullets from the magazines and place them into special wooden blocks which had 40 holes drilled for the pistol rounds and 50 for the machine gun rounds, before they were returned to the duty armourer.

If any of the holes in the block remained unfilled it meant that bullets were missing … and that meant big trouble.

Of course, at the end of the evening shift there was always a scramble to get off duty, hand in radios, ammunition and weapons and get off to the police club for *last orders*.

Steve recalls that during one such evening shift a number of the corporals had upset the shift sergeant by messing about. Anyway, at the end of the shift the sergeant gathered his men together before beginning the disarming procedure and said, "Right chaps because some of you have been naughty boys with the *Sarge* this evening, here is a little competition and the winner goes off duty first... OK, you must beat me and complete twice as many as I do."

The sergeant then demonstrated that he wanted his men to clench their fingers into a tight fist and squeeze for a few seconds before unclenching and stretching their fingers.

The sergeant then did over 100, meaning that his young scallywags had to do 200.

When they had finished he ordered them all to unload their weapon magazines and place the bullets into the wooden blocks.

Unfortunately, after all the clenching and stretching, their fingers were as much use as *chocolate fire-guards*. It was as if their fingers had been dipped in *Novocaine*.

The sergeant laughed so much that his men realised he had won the day. Although they made *last orders* in the club that evening, from that day on, whenever his chaps started to get out of line, all the sergeant had to say was, 'Finger exercises at the end of the shift chaps?'

Drawn by Flight Sergeant 'Shep' Shepherdson

DOUBLE VISON

Billy King

At Laarbruch in the late '70s part of the unit's anti-drink driving campaign called for all drivers leaving the unit after 2200 hours to stop their vehicles at the main gate and report to the police post to *book out,* providing their rank, name, unit, car registration and the time. The clipboard with the forms was situated on a ledge outside the police post enquiry window facing onto the clock on the back wall. For the RAF Police NCOs on duty at the main gate it was an ideal way of observing each driver for any evidence of drunkenness as he or she walked from their vehicle and completed the details in the book. Drivers found to be *under the influence* would be refused exit and would be compelled to hand their vehicle keys over to the police until they were sober. Those who were un-cooperative were usually dealt with officially.

Anyway, one evening I was on duty at the gate with Corporal Steve Davies when we came up with a super wheeze. Firstly, we turned the clock on the wall upside down (as it didn't actually have numbers displayed, one had to look twice to see that something was odd). Secondly, after putting out the clipboard with slightly fuzzy photocopied forms, Steve and I stood close to the police post swaying slightly from side to side in unison.

Of course, when the first few customers arrived to book out they were faced with two policemen who seemed to be swaying ... or was it them?

Then, of course, they started filling in the form ... was in blurred, or was it them?

Finally, as they looked up to the clock to record the time, they were again not sure what was wrong... Was it the clock, or was it them?

Most said nothing, but quickly referred to their wristwatches instead.

As they left with "Goodnight lads" we both, still swaying in unison, responded with, "Goodnight sir (or madam), drive safely".

I wonder how many of them questioned just how much they had consumed that evening as they drove home...

Drawn by 'Robbie'

TOUGH CUSTOMERS

Michael O'Neill

RAF Colerne 1961: The first indications that the Saturday night shift might not to be as quiet as normal came when a phone call to the guardroom complaining about unruly behaviour was made by the manager of the Astra Cinema. He was insistent that the RAF Police should restore good order before he allowed the main film to be screened.

Mitch, the duty policeman, arrived at the cinema a few minutes later. The first ten rows were occupied by Army personnel, more precisely a contingent of SAS (*Special Air Service*). Mitch called for the house lights and proceeded to the stage, from where he informed the unruly mob that they were guests of the RAF and that they should appreciate that the cinema was an amenity utilised by everyone, including families.

Fortunately, there was a SAS officer amongst the group and he understood what had been said. Everyone quickly quietened down and the film started.

Mitch, quite pleased with himself for handling a potentially tense situation well, returned to the guardroom, thinking smugly to himself, '*He who dares wins*'.

As a matter of routine, he logged the incident into the police occurrence book and informed the guard commander and the Orderly Sergeant as a matter of course. He also contacted Charlie, the dog handler out on patrol, and asked that he keep the guardroom informed of his whereabouts, just in case.

At 2130 hours the telephone rang. It was the NAAFI manager, screaming down the phone that the Army was wrecking the place.

As Mitch reassured the manager that he was on his way, he put the phone down and his mind raced through what he had been taught to do in such circumstances. He quickly contacted the Orderly Officer and Orderly Sergeant and requested their presence. He then contacted Charlie and asked him to make his way to the front of the NAAFI and await their arrival.

Within minutes, the Orderly Officer, a young pilot officer who hardly looked old enough to shave, let alone command, arrived and asked for a briefing. Mitch calmly explained that the SAS were apparently wrecking the NAAFI. The pilot officer responded by asking Mitch what they should do. Mitch suggested that the presence of a RAF officer flanked by two RAF Policemen should be enough to calm everyone down.

"Right," said the pilot officer. "As soon as the Orderly Sergeant arrives we'll go and sort them out".

Within minutes the Orderly Sergeant arrived and was briefed en route to the NAAFI.

Outside the NAAFI the four intrepid heroes and a police dog gathered for the kill.

"Right then corporal," said the pilot officer. "What's the plan of action?"

"Well, if you would like to walk inside sir," replied Mitch, "the dog handler will be on your right and I'll be on your left. The very sight of an officer should quieten them down and the sight of the dog should sober them up."

The theory was brilliant, but something went wrong with the execution, because as they marched purposefully through the doors and inside, the pilot officer remained outside.

He might have been young, he probably still didn't shave, but stupid he certainly was *not*!

All the tables in the bar had been pushed together to form a huge platform and several of the SAS soldiers, to the delight of the others, were doing impersonations of *Fred Astaire* on the tables. Glasses were all over the place: full, half full, empty and broken. Raucous singing and ribald comments assaulted the ears.

"Right Charlie," said Mitch, "Lets get the two biggest, they're the ringleaders. Sort them out and the rest will be like pussy-cats."

Again, the theory was sound; in fact, it was a good plan.

The two policemen and the dog rushed the tables and attempted to arrest the ringleaders. However, in the next instant all three were outside again, having been thrown out of the windows.

Amazingly, none of them had been hurt.

The pilot officer and Orderly Sergeant were stunned by the spectacle and just as they were gathering for another frontal assault, the SAS officer came out to check if they were alright. He then apologised for his men's 'good natured tomfoolery' and requested ten minutes for his men to clear up and retire for the night.

The four intrepid heroes were amazed but the officer was as good as his word and after ten minutes the SAS were lined up outside and off they went, marching down the road to bed.

"Well," said the pilot officer. "We seem to have handled that situation rather well, corporal. I suggest you give them fifteen minutes or so and then check on their accommodation."

"Thank you sir," replied Mitch, "I'll do just that after I've taken the dog handler and his dog back to the kennels. Good night sir."

The poor old dog was unharmed but still hadn't worked out what had happened to her, but to be fair, neither had Charlie or Mitch, everything had happened in a blur.

After leaving the dog to settle in her kennel, Mitch and Charlie made their way to the transit accommodation being used by the SAS. As they approached they saw mattresses strewn over the grass outside and hanging from open windows, but all was quiet. Inside, there were men fast asleep on bare wire bed frames, on the floor and even on top of lockers. All were fully dressed in their full battledress combat uniforms and all were cuddling their rifles.

There was no further trouble that night and the SAS were airlifted out at 0400 hours that morning to who knows where.

No wonder 'Who Dares Wins' is the motto of the SAS.

"But Dinwiddy, that hairdo just isn't you!"

Drawn by 'Dusty' Miller

A BRILLIANT SHINE

Madge Joseph (nee Chapman)

At Netheravon in the early 1960s the trainee dog handlers at the RAF Depot suddenly started to ask the WRAF kennel maids for their 'RAF issue' sanitary towels, which apparently were brilliant for cleaning the windows in preparation for the weekly inspections during the period leading up to the 'annual formal inspection' of the station by the Air Officer Commanding.

At the time, of course, the station Supply Officer and his staff had no idea why the WRAF were suddenly going through so many, and being men, were no doubt far too embarrassed to ask.

I suppose had they plucked up enough courage to ask the question, the reply they would have received from the kennel maids may well have been something like:

"Don't worry, it's just a difficult period we are going through at the moment..."

Apparently, they were also brilliant for cleaning shoes.

"I said attack me, blast you, attack me"

Drawn by 'Roberts'

"About turn—double—and get them skids on!"

Drawn by Flight Sergeant 'Shep' Shepherdson

STRICTLY NO ENTRY

Boris Durham

At a time when relations between the British and the Egyptians were not particularly good, Corporal Durham was the senior RAF Police NCO on duty in the guardroom one night at 107 Maintenance Unit in the Suez Canal Zone.

It was one of those rare occasions when it rained; in fact, there had been quite a deluge. As the downpour subsided, one of the gate sentries came into the guardroom and reported that there were three cars at the gate and the drivers were asking for permission to pass through the base to get to the Canal Road because the parallel Treaty Road was blocked by floodwater and sand.

For two reasons Corporal Durham refused permission; the first being that the access gate onto the Canal Road was locked at dusk and the second that they were Egyptian civilian vehicles which were not allowed onto the British military base.

As the sentry left to pass on the decision of his supervisor, Corporal Durham continued to drink his tea and the rest of the shift passed by without further incident.

The following morning, however, Corporal Durham was summoned to see the station commander to explain why he had refused permission for the three cars, one of which had contained Egypt's King Farouk, to take a shortcut through the base.

Corporal Durham was at a loss for words, but as he was dismissed, the station commander smiled and suggested that he might be a little more diplomatic in the future.

Artist unknown

JUST WINDOW SHOPPING

Steve Cattell

Whilst serving at RAF Northolt on the Western edge of London, I recall that one day a dog handler didn't secure the padlock properly on one of the dog kennels and as a result the dog got out and went on a walkabout.

The Station Commander was doing his nut when he heard; after all, RAF Northolt was in the middle of a built up area and he was extremely worried that something terrible might happen, such as a child being attacked, etc.

We finally got a telephone call that the Alsatian had been seen walking down the middle of Harrow High Street and when we got there that is exactly what was happening.

It was just like one of the films you see of an escaped zoo lion walking calmly along the road with a police car slowly following behind it.

The dog, of course, was rather curious, because he had never seen traffic or real people before and all the shops were definitely a whole new experience.

Driving the RAF Police vehicle, accompanied by a dog handler, I overtook the civil police car and pulled in front of the dog. We then opened the front passenger door of the Ford Escort estate (which, incidentally, had no front passenger seat because it had broken and hadn't been replaced) the 'wild beast' calmly jumped straight in, licked our faces, curled up on the back seat next to the handler and went to sleep, relieved and safe after his first experience of High Street window shopping.

Drawn by 'Angel'

NOT DEAD YET

Stephen R Davies

During one of my tours of duty at Rudloe Manor, we had a warrant officer living in the mess who, by virtue of the important job he was involved with, had been allowed to extend his service by a year over that normally required for retirement; even so, he was still only fifty-six.

After taking lunch in the mess, this particular warrant officer would normally retire to his favourite armchair in the ante-room to read his newspaper and take a short nap before returning to his office for the afternoon. It was a regular routine and no-one was surprised to see him slumped in the armchair snoozing with his large *spreadsheet* covering his head.

I recall one lunchtime when he was in the armchair, snoozing as usual; no-one took any special interest and people came and went as normal. However, after work that day, I, along with a few others, returned to the ante-room to read the newspapers and drink some tea. We were rather surprised to see the warrant officer still slumped in his armchair at that late hour, seemingly fast asleep and covered by his newspaper.

At first there were a few humorous comments made, but then we grew concerned. Had he been there since lunchtime? Was he Okay? We warily approached and called out his name...

There was no response and he didn't appear to be breathing.

We tried calling him once again but slightly louder and with more urgency in our tone... still there was no response.

"Oh my God," someone said, "Has he expired?"

Cautiously, we pulled away the newspaper to see if he was still alive and were dumbstruck to discover that some scoundrel had placed a tailor's mannequin in the armchair. The real warrant officer was perfectly well but away from the unit on duty for a few days.

The mannequin, I might add, was used most successfully over the coming weeks to surprise a number of other people in various situations, but those are stories for another time!

"Steady chaps, this is it! Sogcroft, Oddbody, Dewslip, you take the WAAF riding the bike without lights, we'll tackle the airman not wearing his hat"

Drawn by 'Dusty' Miller

SERGEANT POWER

Author Unknown

Eleven people were dangling below a helicopter on a rope: ten RAF provost officers and one RAF Police Sergeant.

Since the rope was not strong enough to hold all the eleven, they decided that one of them had to let go to save all the others but they could not decide who should be the volunteer.

Finally, the Sergeant said he would let go of the rope, since Sergeants are used to doing everything for the good of the Service. They forsake their family, don't claim all their expenses and do a lot of overtime without getting anything back in return. When he finished his moving speech all the provost officers began to clap...

Never underestimate the power of a RAF Police Sergeant.

A group of provost officers and a group of RAF Police Sergeants take a train to a conference. Each officer holds a ticket but the entire group of Sergeants has bought only one ticket for a single passenger. The officers are just shaking their heads and are secretly pleased that the arrogant Sergeants will finally get what they deserve.

Suddenly, one of the Sergeants calls out.

"The conductor is coming!"

At once, the Sergeants jump up and squeeze into one of the toilets. The conductor checks the tickets of the officers. When he notices that the toilet is occupied he knocks on the door and says, "Ticket, please!"

One of the Sergeants slides the single ticket under the door and the conductor continues merrily on his round.

For the return trip the officers decide to use the same trick and buy only one ticket for the entire group, but they are baffled as they realize that the Sergeants didn't buy any tickets at all.

After a while one of the Sergeants announces,

"The conductor is coming!"

Immediately all the officers race to a toilet and lock themselves in. The Sergeants leisurely walk to the other toilet, but before the last Sergeant enters the toilet, he knocks on the toilet occupied by the officers and says, "Ticket, please!"

And the moral of this story is ~ Provost Officers like to use the methods of their Sergeants, even if they don't really understand them.

Once upon a time three provost officers were walking through the woods when suddenly they were standing in front of a huge, wild river but they desperately had to get to the other side.

How could they do it with such a raging torrent?

The first officer knelt down and prayed to the Lord.

"Lord, please give me the strength to cross this river!"

Pppppffffffffuuuuffffffff! The Lord gave him long arms and strong legs so that he could swim across the river. It took him about two hours and he almost drowned several times, but he was successful!

The second officer, who observed this, prayed to the Lord and said, "Lord, please give me the strength AND the necessary tools to cross this river!"

Pppppffffffffuuuuffffffff! The Lord gave him a tub and he managed to cross the river despite the fact that the tub almost capsized a couple of times.

The third officer, who observed all this, knelt down and prayed, "Lord, please give me the strength, the means and the intelligence to cross this river!"

Pppppffffffffuuuuffffffff! The Lord converted the officer into a RAF Police Sergeant. The Sergeant took a quick glance on the map, walked a few meters upstream and safely crossed the river using the footbridge.

I'm sure you can come up with your own moral!

TRULY BOUND OVER

Stephen R Davies

I was on night patrol when my radio crackled into life, to inform me that the duty medical orderly required urgent assistance at the station medical centre. Apparently, he had complained that a violent drunken soldier was causing a disturbance there.

We responded, but I was worried about my partner, Matt McCarthy, who had received what looked like a painful back injury during a rugby match earlier in the day. He shouldn't have been on duty really but he was as stubborn as a mule.

Anyway, I told him that if we encountered any trouble he was to stay out of it and just call for backup. The unit that the soldier belonged to, had a reputation of 'no surrender' and fighting it out until the bitter end!

We arrived at the scene a few minutes later and entered the building. Strangely, everything seemed very quiet. I called out for the medic and he came out from a side-room. I asked if he had called for assistance and he confirmed that he had.

When I asked if the soldier had gone, he said that he hadn't and indicated for us to follow him into the room which he had appeared from.

We walked in and were absolutely speechless at the sight before us. There was the soldier, lying on the floor, tied up with bandages and looking rather like an Egyptian mummy! He wasn't very happy with his situation and was cursing through a gag around his mouth and struggling like hell to get free.

I asked the medic if he had tired the soldier up and he confirmed that he had to because the soldier was getting 'boisterous'. I looked at the medic, who didn't look as if he had it in him, and smiled.

Anyway, the soldier was obviously drunk, so he was put into the back of our Land Rover, still struggling to get free.

Matt, for all his aches and pains, was killing himself laughing at the scene before him.

Soon afterwards, we took our prisoner into the guardroom and handed him over to the duty sergeant, who looked totally surprised. After some very quick explaining the soldier was cut free and placed into one of the cells to sober up.

He certainly wasn't a 'happy chappie' – that we could tell.

"There, there, Bertram, we'll look again; I'm sure there must be something we can 'ave him for!"

Drawn by 'Dusty' Miller

MUNRO MAJOR

Stephen R Davies

In 1978 RAF Laarbruch in Germany, close to the Dutch border, was a very busy and important NATO frontline base in the *Cold War* against the Soviet air forces deployed less than twenty minutes flying time away behind the *Iron Curtain*.

At the time, the RAF Police Squadron at Laarbruch was under the command of a rather unpredictable and somewhat eccentric squadron leader who, prior to transferring into the Provost Branch, had apparently been an Army tank commander. His radio call-sign was *Munro Major* and whenever he was on the prowl or came on the radio his men would literally quake; such was the nature of the man.

One afternoon, the radio within the Security Control Centre, crackled into life and *Munro Major's* voice boomed out.

"*Munro Control* this is *Munro Major*, over."

For a few seconds the police controller froze.

"*Munro Control* this is *Munro Major*, do you read me? Over."

The control room went silent as the controller responded.

"*Munro Major* this is *Munro Control* send your message, over."

"*Munro Control* this is *Munro Major*, I'm out in my vehicle and I can see three helicopters flying near the airfield. What are they doing? Over."

The controller looked stunned and looked towards the sergeant for guidance. The sergeant responded sarcastically by saying something like, "This is an airfield for God's sake! What does he suppose they're doing?"

At that point, the radio crackled into life again with some urgency and it was clear that the squadron leader was getting annoyed.

"*Munro Control* this is *Munro Major.* Did you receive my last message? Over."

The controller, trying to conceal the amusement in his voice, responded, "*Munro Major* this is *Munro Control*, we copied your last transmission and are checking. Standby, over."

At that point, joking aside, the sergeant knew that the squadron leader was deadly serious. He sent one of his men outside with a pair of binoculars to see what was happening in the air and telephoned air traffic control to enquire what the helicopters were doing.

At first the duty air traffic controller was just a little confused as to why the police should want to know what the three helicopters were doing, but when the sergeant explained, the controller sympathetically reassured him that there was nothing wrong; the three Dutch helicopters were just passing the unit and were not intending to land.

The sergeant quickly passed the information to the radio controller, who started to transmit.

"*Munro Major* this is *Munro Control*, message, over."

"*Munro Control* this is *Munro Major,* send your message, over."

"*Munro Major* this is *Munro Control,* air traffic control confirm that the helicopters are just passing by and do not intend to land here, over."

Just as the sergeant was thinking that was the end of the matter, the squadron leader responded.

"*Munro Control* this is *Munro Major,* that's all very well but why did none of your men report this? Ensure that your men are alert to such things from now on; this could quite easily have been an invasion by special forces. Out."

With that, a very confused sergeant came on the radio to address his men deployed at various points on the unit.

"*Munro Control* to all call-signs. All suspicious aerial activity occurring around the airfield is to be reported immediately, acknowledge, over."

In response, each call-sign on the radio net acknowledged the instruction, but for many days afterwards, almost every aircraft movement, and there were many, was being reported as suspicious.

Hardly surprisingly, the air traffic controllers thought that the police had completely lost the plot!

Common sense did, however, eventually prevail, but *Munro Major* remained as unpredictable and as eccentric as ever, as this next story will show.

Munro Major's private vehicle was a white long wheel-based hard-top Land Rover in which he used to 'patrol' the unit. As a result, he quickly became known as *Daktari,* after a television program about a safari gamekeeper who used a similar vehicle out in the African bush.

During the monthly 'war game exercises' all the RAF Police Land Rovers, which were already painted a ugly matt green colour, were camouflaged using netting onto which artificial foliage was attached. The camouflage was so fitted, that it remained in place while the vehicles, looking like bulky shrubs, were mobile.

On one such occasion, everyone was highly amused to see *Daktari* driving around in his Land Rover, swathed in green camouflage netting. The camouflage, however, did little to disguise his gleaming white Land Rover beneath.

After parking briefly outside the Security Control Centre, where his vehicle quickly became the focus of various comments, *Daktari* had started to reverse out of the parking slot when the camouflage netting around his vehicle became entangled in a fire tender and resulted in both of his wing mirrors being ripped clean off.

Unfortunately, it was shift change-over at the time and the giggles coming from the great multitude of RAF Police corporals gathered in the car park could hardly be contained.

Daktari removed the camouflage netting from his vehicle shortly afterwards and never used it again.

"He's the best blinking dog handler on the unit"

Drawn by 'Clayton'

THE DENTAL INSPECTION

Stewart McArdle

It was around mid 1984 at RAF Waddington when Flight Sergeant Brian Denman, the NCO in charge of the Security Office, received a memo from the Dental Section saying that he had not been in for a dental inspection since his arrival on the unit many months before.

Now Brian was getting rather annoyed with the dental staff because he had informed them soon after arriving that he had a full set of false teeth, so once again he ignored the memo.

However, after a few more weeks another memo arrived, more or less threatening that if he did not appear for his dental appointment then his commanding officer would be notified and formal action would be taken against him.

So what did Brian do under such provocation?

Well, he produced the spare set of his dentures, which he duly placed in a small box, together with a memo of his own, stating that the enclosed teeth belonged to Flight Sergeant Denman and were reporting for their dental inspection as ordered.

The memo also asked for the teeth to be returned once the inspection had been carried out.

A day later, the teeth were duly returned, together with a rather witty memo from the Station Dental Officer, confirming that all was well.

Common sense prevailed thereafter!

"I often wonder whether you married me
or the Air Force!"

Drawn by Flight Sergeant 'Shep' Shepherdson

SOUTHERN FRIED JUSTICE

John Law

In 1964 John was posted to the AIRCENT International Police Unit, based at Camp Guynemer in France. However, when France opted out of the military aspect of NATO the headquarters were re-located to Hendrick's Mine outside Brunnsum in the Netherlands. AIRCENT and AFCENT were amalgamated to form the AFCENT International Police Unit and for the first time the RAF Police found themselves working with American Military Police and the Dutch Royal Police, otherwise known as the *Koninklijke Marechaussee.*

Because of the disparity between national ranks graded according to the American military structure, British corporals were designated as OR4; sergeants as OR5 and flight/staff sergeants became OR7. By tradition, the post of Provost Sergeant had been held by a United States Air Force (USAF) master sergeant (OR8), but the United States Army had the audacity to post in a top sergeant (OR9) which made him the ranking NCO. The USAF quickly retaliated by posting in a chief master sergeant (OR10), which preserved their hold on the prestige post.

It turned out that Chief Master Sergeant Tuggle was a *good-ole Southern redneck* and he quickly put his stamp on the organisation by issuing a number of edicts, one of which stated that no-one under the grade of OR5 could make an arrest without his permission. That posed a few problems because, with the exception of the German NCOs who had been graded OR5, most of the working military police were OR4s.

One night on the graveyard shift, John returned to the police station from patrol to be greeted by an unruly drunken British airman, who was, for some reason, wearing Scottish highland dress and waving his dirk (ceremonial dagger) across the counter at the Sergeant of the Guard (a USAF OR5), who was cowering in the far corner of the room.

Acting on instinct, John disarmed the drunk, arrested him, bundled him into the patrol car and drove him to the Maastricht Detachment, as there were no holding cells at Brunnsum. Once there, John lodged the necessary paperwork at the RAF Detachment HQ and happily went home after his shift ended.

It was mid-morning when he was woken by his wife, who informed him that the police wanted to talk to him. At the door were two United States Army Military Policemen, resplendent in their dress uniforms, who told him that the Provost Sergeant required his immediate presence.

When John arrived at the Provost Sergeant's office, the *good-ole Southern boy* was leaning back in his chair and asked John if he had arrested anyone during the night and on whose authority had he done so.

John replied that he had and had been granted the power of arrest under British Air Force Law and the Queen's Regulations, so his ultimate authority came from Her Majesty the Queen.

The *good-ole Southern boy* took another chew on his tobacco before uttering the immortal words, "I'm rescinding her authority. You are suspended pending an investigation. Turn in your badge and your gun." As John was about to leave his office, the *good-ole Southern boy* added, "And get over to Maastricht and get that guy out of jail."

John thought the *good-ole Southern boy* would have apoplexy when he replied, "Sorry, but she only gives me the power to jail them, not bail them."

On the way out of the Police Office, John bumped into Squadron Leader Joe McLean, a RAF provost officer, who held the appointment of Assistant Provost Marshal (APM). When he asked John why he was there John unfolded his story.

Afterwards, the APM told John to stay where he was and went in to see the Provost Sergeant. Within half an hour John was fully reinstated and his badge and gun were returned. His relationship with the Provost Sergeant, however, was never the same and he was glad that his tour of duty with NATO was nearing its end.

A REALLY BENT COPPER

Stephen R Davies

Dedicated to the memory of George Crawford, who was killed on duty in Germany in February 1985 with members of the RAF Germany Band and their German coach driver.

George Crawford was a rather stocky RAF Policeman and rugby player who came from Liverpool. He sported a walrus type moustache and possessed a wicked sense of humour.

I was on duty with him one evening, and was going in for a cup of tea. As I got out of the car, a dog handler, Mick, and his dog Simba, came around the corner. I bent down to stroke the dog and something in my back clicked loudly and I couldn't straighten up. It was quite painful and I pleaded with Mick to call me an ambulance.

Thinking I was *taking the Mickey*, he replied, 'Okay, you're an ambulance.'

I started to laugh and that made things worse.

George was called but just added to the comments with:

'I can't stand bent coppers' and 'Do you want to me to lend you a pound until you get straight?'

It was obvious that they were enjoying themselves but at last I convinced them that I was serious and they duly summoned an ambulance.

Unfortunately, the one that the Medical Centre sent over was a Land Rover crash ambulance and in my condition it was hard work trying to get into the high back door.

Needless to say, as I tried, everyone was killing themselves laughing at my predicament.

I finally made it and was subsequently taken to the Medical Centre and the medical officer was called out to see me.

George managed to keep the jokes going until the doctor arrived some fifteen minutes or so later.

I wasn't sure whether the pain was coming from my back or from all the laughing that George had me doing.

After being examined, George and the doctor lifted me up so I could hold onto the top of a door frame. Not an easy job!

They slowly lowered me and my back clicked back to normality. I was then subjected to a heat lamp and a fantastic massage at the hands of a rather good looking nurse.

So I suppose I had the last laugh of the evening after all!

Drawn by Flight Sergeant 'Shep' Shepherdson

A DOG AT THE MOVIES

Jeff (Robbie) Robinson

An airman went along to the camp cinema one evening. The film was just starting when he sat down. As his eyes adjusted to the dark, he suddenly noticed a RAF Police dog handler and his dog sitting just along the row from him. He was somewhat bemused but decided to try and ignore the dog and turned to watch the screen.

As the film progressed however, the airman noticed that the dog was reacting appropriately to the various scenes; for laughter the dog wagged his tail and barked; for sadness he dropped his ears and whimpered; for violence the dog growled and bared his teeth. It was quite remarkable.

At the end of the film the audience applauded and the dog stood up on his back legs, barked excitedly and wagged his tail.

The airman, unable to hold back any longer, turned to the dog handler and said,

"Wow, that was a great film, and what an intelligent police dog you have there; frankly, I'm amazed."

"So am I," replied the dog handler. "He absolutely hated the book."

"Oh yes, they're devoted to each other"

Drawn by 'Clayton'

BUZZ OFF!

Stephen R Davies

While I was serving as a sergeant at RAF Marham in 1983, one of my senior corporals wanted to specialise and become a personal protection officer ~ or 'bullet catcher', as we called them.

Billy Newbigging seemed very set on that line of work and I had no doubt that he would make a very capable contribution in that area. However, later on, I discovered something that gave me reason to reconsider my professional opinion.

It happened one day as we were walking back to the car after doing some shopping. A wasp was flying around him and he obviously hadn't noticed it.

I mentioned it to him and the reaction was incredible.

Suddenly, his shopping and an ice cream he was eating were abandoned in mid-air and he took off down the car park, waving his arms like a demented windmill, screaming at us to get it off him.

I remember watching the reaction of two little old ladies who were surprised and somewhat confused by his antics.

I'm afraid I couldn't do anything to assist, as I was doubled up with laughter.

Afterwards, we learnt that Bill really did have a genuine fear of wasps, armed or unarmed!

Drawn by Derek Knight-Messenger

A WINDY WIND-UP

Stephen R Davies

RAF Police morale on B Shift at Marham in 1983 was very high. I suppose as a result of this situation, the odd practical jokes were inevitable – and some of them were very odd indeed.

Now, for some reason, whenever I've worked on a night shift, I have always liked to eat mature cheddar cheese sandwiches. On one particular night I had just prepared a beauty, when I was called into the operations room, to take a telephone call. When I returned, I settled down to enjoy my sandwich, along with a nice cup of tea.

After about twenty minutes or so, I suddenly began to develop a sudden build up of gas in my gut, to the extent that it was uncontrollable. As a result, I had to rush off to the toilet to seek relief.

I returned to the operations room and the same thing started to happen again. Once again, I visited the toilet, only this time, when I came out, I detected one or two giggles from personnel working in the operations room, but took no real notice.

However, when the gas built up for a third time, I became worried and, as I dashed off again, the giggling increased.

Afterwards, I became suspicious and discovered that a certain powder, which caused the sudden build up of gas, had been purchased from a local joke shop by Billy Newbigging and added to my sandwich, while I was on the telephone.

Although I saw the funny side of the joke, it took several hours for my system to fully recover from the ordeal!

Drawn by 'CDR'

PAYBACK TIME

Stephen R Davies

Some weeks after the 'gas attack', I visited the local joke shop and saw to my delight that they sold small replica 'wasps'.

Yes, you are already ahead of me on this one!

Well, Billy Newbigging had come in to the control room for a cup of tea and had left his webbing belt on a side table. While his back was turned I quickly fastened one of the 'wasps' to the shoulder strap of the webbing belt and stood back.

After Bill had finished his break he replaced his jacket, put on his webbing belt, picked up his sub-machine gun and was heading towards the door.

At that point I shouted out to him that there was a wasp on his shoulder.

He immediately turned and, disbelieving me, shouted back, 'Yeah, yeah!'

However, as he did so, he saw the wasp and immediately turned pale, threw down his gun, had his webbing belt off in a flash and was out the door in one hell of a panic.

The payback had worked!

"You know that all the land in this area belongs to the Air Ministry? —well I have reason to believe that part of it is in your pot."

drawn by Flight Sergeant 'Shep' Shepherdson

A GOOD NIGHT'S SLEEP

Mike Olney-Smith

Background to this story: The larger than life 'Cattigan' (identical) twins, Mick and John, joined the RAF Police in 1951 and quickly gained a reputation of working hard and playing even harder. They loved rugby and beer and served most of their career together. On one occasion in Aden in 1953 they were forced to arrest a very drunk and disorderly Private William Speakman VC of the Black Watch Regiment, who had been awarded the Victoria Cross whilst serving in Korea; the first and only time that a VC holder has been arrested by the RAF Police.

Later, in their career, after completing a colourful tour of duty in Singapore, they boarded a troop ship for home and as it sailed past the Tiger Beer Brewery, the flags were lowered in their honour; some even say that the price of shares in the brewery took a substantial drop that week, however...

Place: RAF Police Special Investigation Branch working within West Germany. We had to be in Keil by 0800 hours the following morning to meet the boss and representatives of the German Criminal Police (Kripo). It was already 2200 hours and we were in a bar on the *Reeperbahn* in Hamburg's red light zone. Mick Cattigan was in good form and was conducting an *Oompah* band for the umpteenth time... I just wished that one of the Germans could sink a stein of beer quicker than Mick and then they would win the privilege of conducting the band and we could leave.

We eventually left the bar at 0200 hours and set off north for Keil. As we made our way out of Hamburg Mick said:

"You drive for the first half hour as I'm tired, then wake me up and I'll take over." No sooner said than done, Mick immediately drifted off into a very deep sleep.

After two hours of driving I could hardly keep my eyes open and tried in vain to wake Mick up. However, despite thumping him and shouting various unpleasant things at him, he continued to snore and nothing it seemed was going to wake him. At the time we were driving along a stretch of autobahn that was still under construction and had just passed under a partly-built bridge when, suddenly, the car shook and there was a tremendous bang. I stopped the car and got out to see what had happened; the bridge we had just passed had collapsed.

Mick had woken up and got out of the car, saying, "What the *(censored)* was that?" When he saw the rubble was only about 400 metres away, he suddenly went quiet, gave me a strange look, then got back in the car and promptly went back to sleep.

I got back in the car and continued to drive but after about thirty minutes or so fell asleep at the wheel. The car careered off the road, spun around and ended up in a field. Surprisingly, I was alright, but all I could see of Mick was his legs in the air and the rest of him buried by our suitcases. He reared up and snapped, "If you want me to *(censored)* drive, just ask!"

The car was alright and we continued our journey without further incident and in the early hours of the morning booked into the hotel. A few hours later when they met up with the boss, Wing Commander G. McClelland, he asked Mick if everything was alright, to which Mick quickly replied, "No Sir it isn't, Olney-Smith has just made two attempts on my life."

drawn by Richard Seal

MINE'S A DOUBLE!

Matthew Geuyen

It was the annual contacts' party at the Headquarters of the RAF Provost & Security Services stationed in Germany.

At the time, Mick Cattigan was serving with the Special Investigation Branch, but his identical twin brother John, who was stationed elsewhere in Germany, was visiting the unit and staying in the Sergeant's Mess.

It was still early evening but as the party progressed, a rather large member of the German civil police by the name of Heinrich issued an open challenge that he could drink any Englishman under the table.

Mick duly stepped forward and accepted the challenge on behalf of the unit and the drinks immediately started to flow.

After a couple of hours, Mick left the bar on the pretext of visiting the toilet, but in reality popped over to the Sergeant's Mess, where he explained the situation to his brother...

Shortly after, John, wearing Mick's clothes, returned to the police club and took up where his brother had left off...

Heinrich, of course, was totally unaware that he had a new drinking partner.

After a few more hours, John left the bar and returned to the Sergeant's Mess, where he woke Mick up for the next phase of drinking... Mick returned to the club and continued to order more drinks for him and Heinrich.

It was sometime just after midnight and although Mick was fairly well, Heinrich was definitely not a sober man.

At that point, John entered the club and stood next to Mick and Heinrich's eyes blinked in disbelief.

Just as he passed out he uttered the words, *"Mein gott im himmel, I'm zeeing da double!"*

Apparently, it took Heinrich a full week to recover from the ordeal; yet another victim of the Cattigan twins!

drawn by Derek Knight-Messenger

DIVING FOR TREASURE

Stephen R Davies

In 1983, a colourful Scotsman by the name of Grant Graham arrived on Ascension Island. As I knew him from a previous tour of duty I knew he was heavily into diving, and indeed he brought his equipment out with him. Apparently, the waters around the island were littered with the wrecks of ships, which hadn't quite made it safely ashore. The existence of these wrecks and what, if any cargo they might have carried, seemed to be a big secret amongst the diving fraternity on the island.

Grant was in his element and soon teamed up with a couple of American divers to explore the waters. As they had been on the island for a lot longer, they knew the coast a lot better and Grant, being a canny Scotsman, took full advantage of that situation.

It wasn't long before they had located a wreck which seemed interesting. Grant was particularly fascinated with the brass port-holes which adorned the hull of the ship, and he was determined to have one. Obviously, that was easier said than done and he therefore assembled the tools he required to cut the port-hole free from the super-structure.

I remember him working on that port-hole for weeks.

He would dive every day and sometimes he would bring up brass letters, which he thought came from the name of the vessel. However, whenever I approached to see what they were, he would quickly cover them up and sneak off. Such was the secrecy of their hobby.

Whenever I asked Grant how work on his port-hole was progressing he would say that it would be free in a couple of days or so.

I waited and waited, until one day, he returned from his dive looking somewhat despondent. When I asked him what was wrong, he showed me the contents of his sack. Inside were two brass port-holes and I looked at him somewhat confused. He then told me that as he was pulling the port-hole free, he had fallen back onto the seabed, disturbing the sand and at the same time, revealing the other port hole, which had been lying there all the time. He went on to say that he wouldn't have minded, but the buried one, was in a far better condition than the one he had spent so much time and effort on.

Well, given the circumstances, I could hardly offer him any sympathy could I?

Several weeks later a group of us, including Grant, were snorkelling in the sheltered English Bay, which at the time was the only safe beach suitable for recreational swimming on account of it being free from the strong undertow current and the presence of sharks. Although there were a lot of spectacular fish in the bay, their presence was outnumbered by the shoals of black trigger fish, which although not harmful to humans, were something like Piranhas whenever food was thrown to them. Indeed, on one occasion, I saw someone throw them a large cabbage which was reduced to a Brussels sprout in seconds.

Anyway, at one point in our snorkelling, Grant started to make a big fuss and we all came up to find out what was wrong. It transpired that he had lost his dental plate whilst adjusting the mouthpiece to his snorkel.

We all rushed over to see if we could help locate his missing dentures and it was no easy task, given all the rocks and gravel on the bottom. After searching with no success for a while we all came to the surface to rethink the search plan.

Suddenly, Grant screamed out that something had just bitten him…

Quick as a flash, I shouted, "It's probably your teeth!"

It was however, just a passing fish, which did no damage.

We did eventually find the dentures, after quite a search.

DOWN MEXICO WAY

Stephen R Davies

During Easter 1984, I was part of a group from RAF Belize who decided to visit the city of Merida in Mexico for a short break.

After a very long journey by coach we eventually arrived in the city just before midnight, and decided to visit a bar which was still open. All thirty of us wandered in and the owner seemed delighted when we all ordered food and beer; no doubt his takings for that night had increased by a few hundred percent.

I remember that at one stage I was sitting at a table, talking to a colleague called Dave when I noticed a rather good looking girl standing near the door looking in our direction. It was obvious that she was interested in one of us from the way she was smiling. I pointed this out to Dave and suggested that I would go to the bar so that we could see which one of us she was interested in.

I got up but had hardly reached the bar before she was sitting in my vacated seat, introducing herself to Dave.

'Ah well,' I thought, 'never mind.' Perhaps it wasn't to be my lucky night after all. I left them to it and joined another group nearby. A little later on, I watched as Dave and the girl left the bar together, hand in hand. 'Well,' I thought, 'at least someone has struck it lucky on our first night in Mexico.'

Later the following morning I bumped into Dave at breakfast and casually enquired if he had enjoyed himself during the previous evening. He gave a wicked smile and said that he had indeed and that she was a *cracking girl*.

I might have been just *ever* so slightly envious but thought no more about it and the subject was dropped.

The remainder of our time in Mexico was really relaxing, and I enjoyed it immensely.

Anyway, I think it was about two days before we were due to leave when we visited the same bar we had been in on the first night. At some point during the evening I again saw Dave's *girl-friend*. This time she wasn't with Dave but with another young airman and they seemed very happy together. She was an attractive girl in her early twenties and had long black hair and a very elegant body. I watched them for a while and sure enough they both left the bar together, arm in arm. I thought that perhaps she might have been a prostitute, but the lad was old enough to know what he was doing and so I thought no more about it.

The following morning, however, while I was at breakfast, I was approached by the same young airman, who looked extremely worried. He apologised for disturbing me and asked if he could have a private word. As this usually indicated someone was in trouble, I agreed.

On the way up to my room, I thought to myself that he had probably been mugged or something similar. When I asked him what was wrong he looked embarrassed and went on to tell me how he had picked up a girl in a bar the previous evening. I quickly established that it was the same girl I had seen him with; the one who had also gone off with Dave on the first night. He then went on to tell me how she had taken him back to her room. After a couple of drinks they started to cuddle and eventually got onto the bed. He became aroused and she started to do pleasant things to him. In due course he prepared to make love to this beautiful girl but, as he started to explore the delights of her body, much to his horror, he found slightly more than he had bargained for.

Yes, the woman was in fact, a man.

Feeling somewhat revolted at what he had discovered, he fled from the room. He looked visibly shocked by the ordeal. I explained that no harm had been done and told him to put it down to experience. He left shortly afterwards, feeling a lot better ... and so did I!

It was a little later in the day when I saw Dave sitting in the hotel bar, having a drink. I decided to join him and the conversation eventually got around to the first evening in the city. I brought up the subject of his lucky first night again and innocently asked for a few more details. He obliged and started to dig himself into a great big hole before my very eyes.

After a while I couldn't contain myself any longer and burst out laughing, wiggling my little finger about in front of him as a gesture to reinforce his compromising position. From the expression on his face, he knew exactly what I was getting at but was stunned and, as soon as he had recovered his composure, wanted desperately to know how I had found out.

I just smiled, rubbed my finger along the side of my nose and explained that it was just good police work. Although he pressed me on a number of occasions after that, he never did find out where the information came from.

I know one thing though; I bet he won't brag about his exploits with women again in such a hurry!

On a subsequent visit to Mexico four years later on my second tour of duty in Belize, a group of us visited the tourist resort in Cancun...

After several hours drinking and making merry in a bar somewhere within the resort, the eight of us had managed to relieve the Mexican waiters of their sombreros and in doing so made a rapid exit from the establishment with the goods.

Having handed over so much of our cash during the preceding hours we thought it only fair to have a souvenir or two to remember the place by!

After a short walk we spotted another bar that seemed to look inviting, however, after a short discussion, I entered it alone, still wearing my hat and walked up to the bar, where I ordered 8 glasses of Tequila, much to the amazement of the barman, who set them up on the bar in front of me. After quickly downing the first glass, the barman stopped to watch me take on the rest. However, I just turned towards the door and in a loud voice called out 'Hi hoe'.

For a few seconds, the place fell silent until from outside came the reply, 'Hi hoe', followed by the entrance of my 7 compatriots, who marched into the bar on their knees one after the other, wearing their sombreros and singing the anthem of the 7 dwarfs; 'Hi hoe, Hi hoe, its off to work we go...'

When they reached the bar, they stood up and downed their waiting Tequilas to a round of applause from the other customers.

All in all, a good night out was had by all in downtown Cancun.

drawn by Steve Davies

THE PARADE

Author Unknown

One day at the RAF Police School there was a big mid-course parade for a high-ranking visiting provost officer. One of the trainee policemen on parade that day was a rather tall and cocky Geordie chap who had already realized that he was not cut out to be a policeman and who had already submitted his application to leave the RAF because he could not cope with the discipline and constant bullshit.

So, there they were, all standing smartly to attention on the parade square being inspected by the high-ranking provost officer, followed by the course instructors,

Suddenly the VIP stopped right in front of Geordie before giving him a careful look up and down and poking him in the chest with his swagger stick.

At that point, he spoke and said, "Well, we seem to have a right scruffy individual at the end of this stick don't we?"

To which Geordie calmly replied, "Yes Sir, but at which end?"

Drawn by Richard Seal

"You know Mavis, there's something awfully familiar about those two!"

drawn by Derek Knight-Messenger

FLUSHED OUT

By Stephen R Davies

While I was at RAF Marham the conversation one day in the Sergeant's Mess centred around the subject of practical jokes. One of the firemen who I was talking to asked if I knew about 'the foam-making compound trick'. I hadn't, and he went on to explain.

"The foam," he said, "used by the airport fire tenders, is created when two separate powder compounds are brought together in water."

"So... how does that help me?" I replied.

"Well," he said. "If one powder is placed in the toilet bowl and the other placed in the water storage tank, whoever flushes the toilet will get more than they bargained for."

"Brilliant!" I said, "When can I have some?"

"Later this afternoon," was the answer.

At the time, my Flight Sergeant was a Scotsman called Gus McGowan and I thought it was about time we played a joke on him. The opportunity came a few weeks later when I had the opportunity to hatch a plan. Luckily, there were two toilet facilities in our police control building; one for the troops and one for the management and operations room staff.

The compounds were duly added to the toilet during the quiet hours of the night shift, when Gus had gone out to check on his troops. The area was then placed 'out of bounds' to everyone else. Gus was always pretty regular in his ablutions and we knew he would visit the toilet sometime before going off duty.

We waited patiently, but the hours seemed to drag by without so much as a *movement* from Gus. We were beginning to give up, when suddenly we saw him disappear in the direction of the toilet with his newspaper.

Quickly and quietly, we all gathered outside the door to await the inevitable.

Again, it seemed like ages before we heard the cistern being flushed.

Initially nothing happened but then, suddenly, there was a loud shriek as Gus, overcome by a sudden build up of foul smelling foam, tried to work out what the hell was happening.

However, I think he quickly worked it out as he heard us all laughing at the door.

At this point, I decided to make myself scarce for a while.

When I did go back, some time later, the cubicle was completely enveloped in foam. Apparently, I had gone a little overboard on the amount of chemicals required.

Luckily, Gus saw the funny side of it, but it took us ages to clean up the mess.

" Could I see the Corporal in charge of the Police, please ? "

drawn by Flight Sergeant 'Shep' Shepherdson

NO SNAKES ON GAN?

Mitch O'Neill

In the early 1970's on the isolated island paradise of RAF Gan in the Indian Ocean there was no fresh milk, no TV, no women and no snakes.

On a quiet afternoon one day the Guardroom telephone rang and when answered the hysterical voice, recognised as Corporal 'Bomber' Burroughs, yelled out that he'd been bitten by snake.

At first the RAF Police NCO on duty didn't react unduly, as Bomber, one of the dog handlers, was known for his sense of humour ~ playing his bagpipes and marching up and down outside the billets at all hours. On top of all that, of course, knowing that there were no snakes on Gan, the RAF Police NCO assumed it was a joke. However, Bomber kept on shouting that he needed help, which finally convinced the Police NCO that something had indeed happened. A patrol was sent over to the dog section, where they found Bomber sat on the ground and alongside him was a dead snake. He had been bitten on the hand and while he had managed to kill the snake, two other snakes had slithered off into the undergrowth.

The Medical Centre was informed but they too didn't believe the story when it was told to them. The RAF Police NCO nevertheless instructed them to contact the Medical Officer and that he was bringing in a rather shocked dog handler.

Placing the snake into a box and Bomber into the Land Rover the patrol rushed over to the Medical Centre. The Medical Officer stated that the snake would have to be identified first so that the correct antidote could be administered, but because there were no snakes on Gan, they didn't have any anyway!

By that stage Bomber was quite pale and, for him, very subdued indeed.

Several anxious hours passed before confirmation was received that the snake was of a non-venomous species. Bomber, needless to say, was quite a relieved and calmer man and didn't play his bagpipes for several days after the incident.

But what about the two snakes that slithered off into the undergrowth?

Well... they were never found, although intensive searches were made.

'No snakes on Gan' indeed!

drawn by John Vitler

NOT SO SOFTLY-SOFTLY

Stephen R Davies

I was on mobile patrol during an evening shift at RAF Laarbruch with a Scotsman called Billy King. We had been parked up quietly watching the world go by when a car drove past us at speed and failed to observe a stop sign. We pulled out, followed and quickly established that it was also exceeding the speed limit.

When we eventually stopped the car, we noticed that the driver was under the influence of alcohol. He agreed to take a breath test and it proved positive. He was arrested and conveyed to the Medical Centre, where the second test confirmed he was over the limit. As a result, he agreed to provide a blood sample for testing, and the Medical Officer was summoned.

It was at this point that a message came over my radio alerting patrols that an intruder had been seen climbing over the perimeter fence into the station. One of the other patrols was despatched and we were asked how long it would be before we could assist. I informed the controller that we were still waiting for the doctor. We were told to report in as soon as we were free. As we waited, it seemed that the intruder had been carrying a bag with him and had disappeared somewhere into one of the wooded areas. As a result, one of the dog handlers had been deployed to the area to assist with the search.

The doctor finally arrived at the Medical Centre and shortly after, our prisoner provided us with the required blood sample.

After handing him over to the duty sergeant in the guardroom, we declared our availability to assist with the search for the intruder. We were tasked to liaise with our Flight Sergeant, known as *Paddy*, at a nearby crash gate.

We quickly made our way there and stopped some distance short of the gate, having switched off our headlights well in advance. Quickly and quietly, Billy and I made our way through the darkness towards the spot were Paddy was waiting for us with another one of our colleagues, *Big Frank* who incidentally, was also an Irishman.

Paddy very quietly updated us on the situation. He told us that a single intruder had been seen by a very reliable witness climbing into the station, close to where the runway approach lights were sighted. Because this was the end of the runway, there were in effect two actual perimeter fences, an inner fence and an outer fence. Accordingly, there was a quarter of a mile sterile area between the two in which the approach lights were situated. In order to allow the emergency services unrestricted access if they needed it, there were two 'crash gates' built into the fences. Our intruder had climbed the outer fence close to where we were holding our briefing. Paddy decided that we were going to open the crash gate and check out the sterile area beyond it for any evidence of our quarry.

He duly produced the key, unlocked the gate and all four of us entered very quietly. By now, my eyes had adjusted to the pitch-black darkness and my ears were alert for every sound on the night air. The area that we were going to check out was a wide stretch of grass and low-lying shrubs, bordered on both sides by thick woodland.

We continued down the track in a kind of leap-frog procession to cover each other in case something happened; well... it all *looked* professional! As we continued to make progress, we made sure that no sound was made and every so often, we stopped to listen out for anything else that might have been moving.

After covering about half the distance, Paddy quietly called us together at the side of the track. He then whispered to Frank, telling him to go back up the track to bring the Land Rover down. Billy and I were slightly puzzled by this, because the engine of the Land Rover would defeat everything we had done for the past half hour or so. However, we bit our tongues and thought that Paddy knew best.

Frank started off very quietly, back up the track and we waited for his return.

It was at that point that Billy and I were frightened out of our wits, as the silence around us was shattered by Paddy, who shouted up the track to Frank, telling him not to switch his headlights on.

As you can imagine, that well and truly compromised our position to any would-be intruder ... and half the bloody base!

We might as well have hung an illuminated neon arrow above us giving our position away to anyone who wanted to know where we were.

Needless to say, we never did find the intruder that night and called the search off soon after Paddy's broadcast to the world.

drawn by Tony Paley

Artist unknown

A WOUND-UP DJ

Stephen R Davies

In 1984 for entertainment in Belize we had a unit of the British Forces Broadcasting Service, based at Airport Camp. Their empire was situated in one of the corrugated huts, from where they presented programs twenty-four hours a day to the troops stationed throughout the country. At the time, they only had one professional presenter, who also happened to be the manager. As such, they were assisted by service personnel who fancied themselves as budding *disc jockeys*.

During my time there one of the part-time presenters was a RAF sergeant called Frank. He always presented the early breakfast show and was extremely good at it. So much so, that I'm sure he had missed out on his true vocation as a professional. I used to wake up every morning during the week, half an hour earlier than I needed to, just so I could listen to his show. It always had me in fits of laughter, even that early in the morning.

Now Frank was a bit of a comedian and the highlight of his show was selecting some poor victim on the camp who had come to his notice for doing something silly. The incident would then be expanded and twisted out of all proportion on the air by Frank, who at the end would reveal the identity of his victim for that day. It was always done in a very funny but humiliating way, with suitable background music to accompany the broadcast. Afterwards, the poor old victim was indeed a true celebrity for the day.

I awoke as usual one morning to hear the show and was rather shocked to discover that it was my turn to be 'victimised'. I listened intently to find out what had brought me to Frank's attention. As it turned out, my blunder was quite a simple mistake really and certainly not worthy of making me famous, or so I thought. However, as usual, Frank exaggerated it out of all proportion just to make it sound more interesting. I wasn't really aware of it before then but the incident happened a few days before when I had been putting together some crime prevention leaflets offering useful advice on how to secure personal belongings etc. Unfortunately, one of the sentences printed onto the leaflet should have read; 'Remember, do not leave your valuables lying about to be stolen'. However, they were circulated with that very important word, 'not' missing from the text, which everyone who read it thought was very amusing. Instead of pointing out this omission to me, they went directly to Frank, and of course he did the rest.

Anyway, Frank gave me hell on the air, in his usual way. Needless to say, my day involved a continuous round of giggles which started as soon as I set foot into the mess that morning for breakfast.

The following morning however, I awoke again as usual and switched on the radio to listen to Frank's show. He played a few records, before moving onto his famous 'victim of the day' spot. I listened with interest as the last record faded away and the famous background music announcing the moment started to kick-in. However, just as Frank was about to speak, he was suddenly stopped in his tracks by a loud knock on the studio door. He apologised for the ill-timed interruption and duly got up and answered the door leaving his microphone open.

Everyone could hear what was happening and as soon as the door was opened we all heard him saying, 'Oh No, not the fuzz'!

At that point, two of my police corporals entered the studio and quite clearly over the air, cautioned Frank that he didn't have to say anything unless he wished to do so, but whatever he said might be used in evidence against him later.

For once he was silent and stuck for words. He then recovered and tried to plead his innocence but was duly arrested for taking the Mickey out of the Sheriff, a truly serious crime.

He was then handcuffed and carted off to jail. Meanwhile, one of my men, who was also a part-time presenter with the radio station, carried on with the last half hour of Frank's show, while Frank was otherwise engaged in a nice comfortable cell.

Yes, as you have correctly guessed, I got my own back on Frank that morning. After all, my credibility was at stake, wasn't it? When I went into the mess for breakfast that morning, a rather large cheer went up from all those assembled, some of whom, had been 'victims' on previous occasions. Obviously, everyone had enjoyed the slight variation to the show.

Frank was later released without charge and had to admit that I'd got one over on him. However, the following morning he was back on the air as usual...

drawn by 'Clayton'

Artist unknown

A ROYAL SUPPER

Stephen R Davies

During 1980, I was part of the RAF Police support team sent to RAF Leeming to enhance security during the period that HRH Prince Andrew was training to become a helicopter pilot. On the first day I was on my way to the mess for lunch with a couple of colleagues. As we were walking up the road we passed a couple of Naval officers and after paying the normal compliments I remarked to one of my mates that one of the officers looked familiar…

"You plonker," he replied. "That was Prince Andrew".

Once settled in, I went on duty one evening and was informed that the prince had driven off the unit in his own vehicle, half an hour earlier and that Inspector Peter Prentice, his personal protection officer [PPO] was in the officer's mess.

I took over the radio, which was a direct link between the prince and his PPO and went for a walk to the main gate. It was a quiet evening, disturbed only by the radio crackling into life. It was the PPO calling the prince. I was somewhat surprised when the prince responded that he was in the fish and chip shop in nearby Bedale. He then asked his PPO if he wanted something bringing back. The PPO replied that he had already eaten. Quite understandably I was somewhat amused by the image of the prince, standing in the queue of a fish and chip shop and hoped that at least that they would wrap his chips in a quality newspaper. However, my thoughts were disturbed by the prince asking if I wanted anything bringing back. I was somewhat stunned and before I could think about it, I heard myself ordering fish and chips from a member of the Royal family!

A short time later, Prince Andrew's Range Rover pulled up at the gate, the window wound down and he handed over my supper. I was still somewhat embarrassed when I asked him how much I owed. The prince however, smiled and replied that it didn't matter.

Well, I thought, how nice, it's not every day that a mere corporal is treated to a fish supper by a member of the Royal family.

By the way, a quality newspaper *hadn't* been used to wrap them...Shame on you, chippy!

"......THEN HE GIVES ME A TANNER AND SAYS,"THIS'LL DO FINE THANKS. THAT WILL BE ALL!"

drawn by 'CHR'

BOMBS OF FRIENDSHIP

Stephen R Davies

In the early 1980s, with so many young acting corporals posted into the police squadron, I designed quite a comprehensive training program to develop their skills as well as assisting the ones straight out of training to pass their promotion examinations. In addition, as the role of the unit had changed with the introduction of two tornado aircraft squadrons there was a considerable amount of training needed to perfect our wartime commitments. To do just that, war scenario exercises were carried out on a regular basis.

I remember that while we were engaged on such an exercise, I was tasked with escorting a convoy of bombs over to No 617 (*The Dambusters*) Squadron. Now at the time, that particular squadron had a formidable squadron warrant officer by the name of Mr McBain. He was a short Scotsman, who, it seemed, had absolutely no sense of humour whatsoever. He ran the squadron with a fist of iron and if anyone got on the wrong side of him, then they were doomed!

The convoy was arranged and we set off for the squadron.

As we arrived at the closed security gates we were stopped by the armed guards and Mr McBain, being the engineering officer on duty, was summoned to accept the weapons.

He came to me first, for clearance to approach the bomb trolleys, and was somewhat amazed when I told him that we had brought the wrong weapons. He immediately checked the paperwork and told me that I was wrong.

Again, I insisted that we were at the wrong squadron and I could see that he was losing his patience.

Again, he checked the paperwork and then the weapon serial numbers and confirmed that they were his. By then, he was not a happy man and demanded to know why I thought they were the wrong weapons. So too did the confused-looking armourers and the policemen, who were also looking on, thinking that I had completely lost the plot.

In response, I turned to him and said, "But look at the *shape* of them!" He looked at them somewhat confused, until I pointed out to him that No 617 (*The Dambusters*) Squadron, normally had those round 'bouncing type' bombs, and that these were just the ordinary conventional bomb shape!

Well, as soon as the penny dropped, he went purple at first, but luckily for me, he eventually broke into a smile.

After that, we got on fine.

"'Ere's Dixon. I can't wait to hear him say 'Evening all'!"

drawn by Flight Sergeant 'Shep' Shepherdson

WELL OUT OF BOUNDS

John Young

The Year was 1960; the place was Nicosia walled city; and the time was just after 0100 hours. Two RAF Police NCOs were on mobile patrol close to the 'Out of Bounds' red light district. They were hot and very thirsty and were just about to go off to find something to drink when into view came a lonely, staggering figure. He was obviously British and obviously a serviceman who seemed more than happy with his night's performance. The two policemen approached the figure and the following dialogue took place:

"And where, young man, are you going?"

"No-where corporal."

"Do you realise that you are out of bounds and breaking the curfew?"

"No corporal."

"Are you Army or RAF?"

"Army corporal."

"Which regiment are you with?"

"Pioneer Corps corporal."

"Which camp?"

"Waynes Keep corporal."

"And what do you do in the Army?"

"I'm with the 14th Mobile Bath & Laundry Unit corporal."

As the two policemen struggled to control their giggles they responded, "Well soldier, it's your lucky night, get in the back of the jeep and we'll take you back to camp."

After dropping the young soldier safely off at his camp, the senior policeman turned to his partner and added, "Well how could we possibly charge a poor little lad doing a job like that?"

His colleague agreed and both NCOs went off giggling in search of that long overdue drink...

"Can't touch her.... works at Air Ministry!"

drawn by Flight Sergeant 'Shep' Shepherdson

THE MASK

Stephen R Davies

During the late 1970s there were a number of rubber face masks on sale in a local joke shop and it just so happened that one of them looked remarkably like our own Flight Sergeant.

As soon as I saw the mask, I couldn't believe just how incredible the resemblance was and an idea began to form in my little grey cells, so I bought one of them.

I took it back to the unit, gave it a slight haircut and then tried it on, whilst wearing my beret. It was incredible really. I went to show two colleagues, Billy King and Tony Hart and they too thought it was fantastic.

Suddenly, my idea started to grow... That night, I took my mask on duty with me and, as luck had it, I teamed up with Tony on mobile patrol. We set off and our first port of call was to visit all the dog handlers on duty at various points around the airfield. As we approached our first target I put the mask on and replaced my beret. Tony brought the Land Rover to a halt and shouted across to the dog handler, telling him that the Flight Sergeant wanted a chat. The dog handler approached to within a safe distance and I took over.

From where he was standing it was obvious that the disguise was working. In my best Irish accent, I asked him if everything was okay and he replied that it was and then I asked how his dog was. Again, he replied that it was okay.

The deception was obviously working very well and we decided to move on in order to try it out elsewhere. I bade the dog handler a good night and we drove off, giggling at the success of our latest prank.

We visited all the dog handlers that night and every one of them really thought I was the Flight Sergeant. I couldn't quite believe just how successful the prank had been, but the best part came later into the shift...

As usual, the 'real' Flight Sergeant decided to go out and visit his troops on their areas of responsibility. Now, this included all the dog handlers. Well, nothing unusual happened until he was about half way through his rounds and a young dog handler, who hadn't been at the unit long, innocently remarked that it was unusual to see him twice in one shift.

As you can imagine, the Flight Sergeant was somewhat confused by the remark. However, instead of investigating further there and then, he returned to the operations room, still looking slightly confused, to ask one of the controllers if he had been out earlier in the night.

Tony and I were in having a tea break at that particular moment almost died laughing and had to quickly leave again.

The poor old Flight Sergeant was even more confused then.

Because the prank had proved so successful, we played it a few more times over the following months until the Flight Sergeant finally worked out what was happening.

Luckily, he managed to see the funny side of it.

drawn by Richard Seal

THE SHOOTING CLUB

Mitch O'Neill

We were in a state of shock! After countless years of mind-numbing security duties, the unit had become 'declassified' in the security sense. The V-Force bomber aircraft that the RAF Police had guarded so meticulously and efficiently were to be pensioned off and their deadly cargoes returned to the United States Air Force. From that point onwards, RAF Marham was officially on a 'Care and Maintenance' footing.

Overnight the RAF Police section shrank from over 125 to roughly 25 personnel. However, the unit administrators still required airfield patrols to be conducted and the three dog handlers were required to patrol the now empty 'bomb dump' just in case some-one should steal it!

The Station Adjutant, now the commanding officer, thought it would be a jolly good idea to form a shooting club, using the redundant airfield as a sort of private estate, with him as the *Squire*. There was always plenty of 'game' about and always had been. The idea seemed extremely viable and so the RAF Police were detailed to be the gamekeepers in this exciting new venture. Pre-selected areas of the airfield were fed with corn every so often to encourage the 'game' into the estate.

The Adjutant stipulated that members of his new club would meet on Saturdays for their newly found 'sport'. However, unknown to the Adjutant, the RAF Police 'poachers club' met on the midnight shift, Mondays through to Fridays. The method they used was slightly more direct and not unlike being on safari. While one man drove the Land Rover around the airfield, his partner would stand up through an opening in the canvas roof and take the game with his shotgun as it was stunned by the glare of the headlights on full beam. Hares, rabbits, partridge and pheasants were easy prey and a local game butcher paid fair prices for the haul, so the midnight safaris were financially rewarding as well.

The Adjutant and the rest of the unit shooting club, however, could never really understand the reason for the shortage of game when they met on Saturdays!

"Oh you are lucky to find him in..... he was due back in camp two days ago"

drawn by Flight Sergeant 'Shep' Shepherdson

SHAIBAH SMITH

Gerald White

Gerald White recalls that, whilst serving at RAF Muharraq in 1969, there was a Scottish dog handler who went by the odd name of 'Shaibah Smith'. Apparently, he had served at RAF Shaibah in Iraq many years before and when relating to an event would always start the sentence with, "When I was at Shaibah..."

'Shaibah' was always telling tall stories, but his colleagues took them all as harmless fun, including his assertion that he was heir to a sprawling lowland estate back home in Scotland.

Indeed, his stories were the *stuff of legend*.

Of course, he also had the capacity to become irritating, especially when he would *absent-mindedly* walk off with a colleague's beer, matches, lighter or sunglasses, but then that was Shaibah.

After a while, some of his colleagues decided that it was time Shiabah was brought to order. The upshot was that a letter was drafted which announced:

> *'Dear Corporal Smith,*
> *I breed Alsatian dogs and need an expert handler here in Manama. I have heard of your expertise in this area and wondered, since you are about to leave the Air Force soon, whether you would perhaps like to work for me.*
> *Your salary and tax free living expenses we could discuss at the interview.*
> *Please come and see me at 38 Pearl Road Manama next Thursday afternoon.*
> *Signed Ali bin Boolsh.'*

The draft was duly given to the Guardroom interpreter to write out in Arabic Script, after which it was posted to 'Corporal 'Shaibah' Smith – Dog handler – RAF Muharraq'.

When the letter duly arrived it was taken back to the guardroom to be translated and Shaibah, having taken the bait, hook, line and sinker, was ecstatic to be offered such a position.

As was his nature, he quickly began showing everyone his fantastic job offer; some indeed twice, and began elaborating in the most extreme terms; at one point he was going to be paid 1000 dinars a week tax-free.

On pay-day Shaibah was seen getting in a taxi for the journey into Manama, the capital of Bahrain, to attend the interview.

Later the same day he reappeared on the base and was astonishingly quiet, and remained so for a few weeks afterwards.

Eventually, someone plucked up the courage to ask him how the job interview had gone, to which Shaibah meekly replied, "Oh, an Army dog handler who could speak the local lingo got the job!"

As you can imagine, there was much stifled laughter as the full story came out.

Still, Shaibah always had that lowland estate back home in Scotland to fall back on!

WHAT'S ALL THIS 'EAR?

Stephen R Davies & Neil Sturtridge

Arriving at my desk on a Monday morning, I was always a little apprehensive about what lay within the mountain of paper-work that had accumulated since cease-work on Friday.

On Monday 30th June 1997 I entered the office as usual and started to sort the papers into different piles: niff-naff; daily situation reports; leave applications; ration returns, shift reports, etc, when suddenly my eyes focused on one of our yellow police evidence labels.

"Strange," I thought. "No-one over the weekend mentioned anything significant happening."

I pulled it from the pile and saw a fleshy-coloured piece of blood-speckled meat within. The label simply declared the contents to be a 'piece of ear'.

By then, I was getting ready to haul someone over the coals for not informing me that a serious assault had taken place over the weekend. Quickly controlling my rising blood pressure, I fished out the relevant police report and started to read:

> 'At RAF Shawbury on 29 June 1997 at 0400 hours, I was on duty in the RAF Police Flight in company with XXX when I witnessed an assault. A person who I now know to be 'Iron' Mike Tyson chased and punched another man, later identified as Evander Holyfield, several times during which he actually bit off a piece of Hoyfield's ear and spat it onto the ground. At the time, a number of American police officers, who had obviously witnessed the assault taking place in the ring, failed to take any action, so I felt that the RAF Police should step in, investigate the matter, and inform the appropriate authorities.'

Yes, I had truly been caught hook, line and sinker by one of my troops who had obviously watched the *Tyson–Holyfield heavyweight boxing match* transmitted live from the States. Realising just how effective the 'wind-up' had been, I quickly decided to include it in the morning briefing to the wing commander in charge of Administration, so off I strolled across to her office.

After the usual greeting, she asked if all was quiet over the weekend. I, in turn, frowned and handed her the evidence bag containing the *meat* and she quickly recoiled and went rather pale. I then related details of the assault and at first she listened intently, with a rather serious expression on her face until suddenly, the *penny dropped!* It has to be said that Wing Commander Lynne Fox also possessed a wicked sense of humour and in response simply said, "Why waste a good wind-up?" and with a smile on her face, whisked the report and the evidence bag into the Station Commander's office to brief him.

Shortly afterwards, Group Captain Alan Waldron, a man who was very pro-police and who also had a healthy sense of humour, summoned the station adjutant, Flying Officer Neil Sturtridge, to a briefing.

In short, the Station Commander agreed that it was indeed a serious matter and one that required a careful examination of the evidence before a decision could be reached on whether to proceed with a prosecution. The adjutant was briefed to produce the summary of evidence and duly locked himself away in his office to draft his report.

After a few days the adjutant submitted his findings to the station commander and his report began:

> 'This is not an easy case... Conflicting evidence suggests that Hoyfield was himself also an aggressor in the fight and did, by his own admission, want to batter Tyson severely about the ring. As such, it is thought that Holyfield is himself a suspect, or on the other hand he could simply be a witness to the assault by Tyson. Accordingly, Holyfield could be a suspect or witness (SOW) in this case. To deal with cases of this nature a Courts Martial should be convened. As it is impractical

for the prosecutor to travel to the USA and also for Tyson and the SOW to travel to the UK, the trial will be conducted by satellite link. Due to the time difference between the USA and the UK it will be necessary for the UK prosecutors to convene the court in the evening, which should not be too problematic. As Tyson and the SOW are professionals, and command vast salaries it is concluded that they will be represented by top US attorneys. In order to counter this, the prosecution wishes to employ the services of a top UK lawyer, preferably a Queen's Council, otherwise known as a Silk. The fees charged by a Silk however, tend to be astronomic and although the station had been requested to provide budgetary support, it was unable to do so. Therefore, alternative sources of funding need to be sought. Bids have been promised from sports memorabilia collectors wishing to see the piece of flesh from Hoyfield's ear which was allegedly bitten off by Tyson, but the sum falls somewhat short of the expected fees. Although all charges may well be proven and a conviction secured, the following conclusion has been drawn: Taking all the above facts into consideration, it has been decided to drop all charges against Tyson as unfortunately,

We cannot make a *Silk's* purse out of a *SOW's* ear!

As to what was actually in that evidence bag?

I shudder to think!

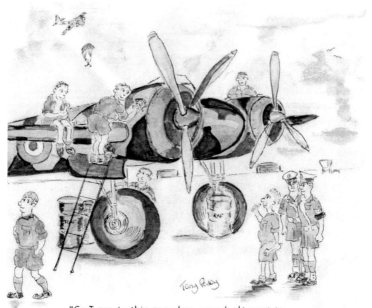

"So I sez to this snowdrop, you don't want to
mess about with us squadron blokes mate"

drawn by Tony Paley

YOGI LOGO

Leslie Bishop

Whilst on detachment to RAF Gibraltar in the mid 1980s, Leslie Bishop, a RAF Police NCO, asked why the *'Gibraltar Air'* flight was always known as 'YOGI' and was told that a number of years before, a certain dog handler, who will remain nameless, had become slightly bored whilst walking his area and so got hold of a set of step ladders, a tin of paint and a brush.

After placing the ladders against the side of the aircraft, he climbed up and painted the letters 'YO' in front of the logo 'GIB AIR' to make it 'YOGIB AIR' (*after Yogi Bear the cartoon character*).

As a consequence, from that day on, the majority of the local people and RAF personnel stationed in the colony referred to the weekly flight as 'YOGI'.

'You came from the sky so you're an airman ...... hand over your 1250 and get put on a charge proper'

drawn by 'Dusty' Miller

Artist unknown

TOM AND JERRY

Stephen R Davies

Because it was so warm at night on Ascension Island I used to sleep with an electric fan switched on in my bedroom, which was located within the police station.

One night I felt something moving about on top of the sheet by my feet. At first, I thought it was the fan blowing against the sheet, but then it happened again...

I switched on the light, looked towards the bottom of the bed and saw a mouse sitting there. I leapt out of bed and of course the mouse did the same and darted off. A chase around the room ensued, with the mouse always in the lead.

At one point I thought I had lost it until, looking around the room, I saw it sitting on the headboard of the bed, staring at me. Again I gave chase but this time it darted behind a large Victorian wardrobe.

By now I was determined to get it and the whole thing started to resemble a *Tom and Jerry* cartoon.

Although the wardrobe was heavy, I managed to move it away from the wall but the mouse just darted off again and hid behind some other piece of furniture. I followed in close pursuit, but the mouse was always one step ahead of me.

At some point a policeman on night duty returned to the station and, on hearing strange noises coming from my room, became alarmed. He banged on the door to ask if I was alright and was amused to hear that I was in hot pursuit of a mouse.

The chase went on for over an hour and it was obvious that the mouse had no means of escape, but by now I was becoming tired ~ so I did the honourable thing. I opened the door and let the little chap escape to freedom.

I looked back at my wrecked room and started to laugh. The duty policeman looked confused as he handed me a coffee...

Standby for Guardroom Tannoy Test..... 1, 2, 3, 4, 5, 6........

drawn by 'Canning'

THE WAY AHEAD

Author Unknown

FACT: In 1999, as part of the *'Provost 2000'* strategy, the Ministry of Defence (MoD) announced major changes to the future role of the RAF Police, in which they envisaged the police trade concentrating on policing and specialist security duties rather than routine armed guarding and basic security duties. The policy changes, agreed by the Air Force Board, meant that routine armed guarding of RAF units would be carried out by all RAF personnel up to the rank of corporal, with the Military Provost Guard Service taking over many of the routine guarding and security duties that had for many years been performed by RAF Police NCOs. It was further announced that over the following two years, the establishment of the RAF Police trade would be reduced to what was described as *'Crisis Establishment Levels'* using natural wastage and reduced recruiting.

FICTION: As a result of the above announcement, the MoD will be forced to reduce the number of serving RAF Police senior NCOs. Under a proposed scheme, older senior NCOs will be asked to go on PVR (Premature Voluntary Retirement), thus permitting the retention of younger people within the branch. Therefore a program to phase out the older senior NCOs by the end of 2003, will be put into immediate effect. The program will be known as 'RAPE' (Retire Aged Personnel Early). Senior NCOs who have been RAPED will be given the opportunity to look for other careers outside the service. Provided that they are being RAPED, they can request a review of their annual assessment reports before actual retirement takes place. This phase of the plan will be known as 'SCREW' (Survey of Capabilities of Retired Early Workers).

All senior NCOs who have been RAPED or SCREWED may file an appeal with PMA (Personnel Management Agency). This will be known as 'SHAFT' (Study by Higher Authority Following Termination). Under the terms of the new policy, senior NCOs may be RAPED once, SCREWED twice, but SHAFTED as many times as PMA deems appropriate.

Senior NCOs who follow the above procedures will be entitled to get 'HERPES' (Half Earnings for Retired Personnel's Early Scheme). As HERPES is considered a benefit plan, any senior NCO in receipt of HERPES will no longer be RAPED or SCREWED by PMA.

Finally, MoD wishes to assure the younger members of the branch who wish to *remain onboard* that they will continue their policy to ensure that you are all well trained through our 'Special High Intensity Training' (SHIT) program. MoD takes great pride in the amount of SHIT you will all receive. Indeed, to date, MoD has given the RAF Police more SHIT than any other branch within the RAF and hopefully will continue to do so well into the future.

drawn by Janner Pascoe

IN THE BEGINNING

Author Unknown

In the beginning there was a Plan,
And then came the Assumption,
And the Assumptions was without form,
And the Plan was completely without substance.

And so it was that the darkness descended upon the faces of the Corporals and the Sergeants who tried to fathom it out.

Totally frustrated, they spoke unto the Flight Sergeant saying, "This Plan is a crock of poo and it stinketh".

Hearing this, the Flight Sergeant did go forth into the Warrant Officer and sayeth, "It is a pail of dung, and none may abide the odour thereof".

The Warrant Officer did deliberate upon the matter and on seeing that it did not compute spake unto the Flight Lieutenant saying, "This plan is a container of excrement and it is very strong, such that none may abide it".

The Flight Lieutenant listened before taking that long walk along the enlightened way to the office of the Squadron Leader where he fell before him saying' "Sir, this is a vessel of fertiliser, and none may abide its strength."

And it did come to pass that the Squadron Leader went onto the Wing Commander and sayeth onto him, "It contains that which aids plant growth, and is very strong."

Hearing this, the Wing Commander did speak soon after to the Group Captain saying, "It promoteth growth and is indeed very powerful."

So, in the fullness of time, the Group Captain did put his name to the Plan and taking it up into the Ivory Tower and before the Air Commodore did say onto him:

"This powerful new plan will actively promote the growth and efficiency of the RAF Police Branch."

The Air Commodore looked at the Plan, and he saw that it was good, and so the Plan became Policy.

And darkness remained upon the faces of the Corporals and the Sergeants.

Amen.

"In the book they just give him an asprin"

drawn by 'Clayton'

SOME LIGHTER MOMENTS

Scott Etheridge

Firstly, I remember the confusion that members of the RAF Police caused to our colleagues in the Army. I was once walking towards the mess tent at RAF Greenham Common when a Major from the *Green Howards* passed us going in the opposite direction. Because he was wearing a para-smock neither I nor Geordie Hindmarsh spotted his camouflaged rank slide and therefore did not salute him. He took great exception to this and rounded upon us, saying, "Don't you salute Majors in the Air Force any more?"

Quick as a flash, Geordie retorted, "But we don't have any Majors in the Air Force sir!"

He was not amused!

The silence was broken late one night at Greenham Common by an anonymous voice saying over the radio,

"Are there any friendly bears out there?"

A few moments passed and then again came,

"Are there any friendly bears out there?"

This went on for about twenty minutes until Warrant Officer Dennis Allen came on the net and announced,

"All call signs, all call signs, this is Warrant Officer Allen, radio discipline will be maintained at all times."

Immediately, a voice replied, "You're not a friendly bear are you?"

Brilliant!

Of course, the following night the same voice re-appeared with, "I'm bored", followed a few minutes later with, "I'm really bored," and then a few minutes after that with, "God, I'm really, really bored." The warrant officer was straight back on the airwaves with, "Last call sign, identify yourself immediately!"

Quick as you like, our hero replied, "I'm not *that* bloody bored!"

The RAF made the mistake of sending a group of RAF Policemen on a Northern Ireland re-enforcement training course at Ballykinler. It was only for a week, but I'm sure it seemed much longer to our poor Army instructors. On the first full morning we were instructed to be on parade by 0730 hours in front of the cookhouse. We duly arrived at 0729 hours only to be screamed at by an irate staff sergeant for being late! When I queried this, the staff sergeant told me that when he said 0730 he meant 0720 as whatever time we were told to be somewhere we should be there ten minutes before, which was standard Army practice.

Of course, it had to happen, just before lunch the staff sergeant barked at us that we had to be back by 1330 hours.

It had to be said, but who would say it?

Suddenly, Colin Vaughan piped up with, "Is that *our* 1330, *the Army's* 1330 or *your* 1330 staff?"

The reply was unprintable.

Later that afternoon we went for a run through open country, during which we were taught how to be 'hard targets' by running about in zigzag lines, apparently so we couldn't be shot at. Of course, the RAF humour came forth once again when one of the guys called out to the Army instructors, "But if we are running, we won't be able to see the nice trees and the pretty birdies."

Guess what? We went for an even bigger run later that day.

Why haven't the Army got a sense of humour?

At RAF Aldergrove our shift turned one entire corridor in the police accommodation into a Santa's Grotto – the only problem was that we did it in October because we couldn't wait! One night shift soon afterwards I was working as the radio operator in the Joint Operations Centre alongside a couple of 'rock apes'

(*RAF Regiment*) who decided that they were going to try and play scrabble! As it came to my turn I put down the word 'fez'.

"What sort of word is that?" enquired one of the rocks.

"It's a hat I said, like the comedian Tommy Cooper used to wear."

Neither of them believed me and therefore they were forced to seek guidance from their duty officer; a young pilot officer. After he managed to persuade them that the word was indeed valid, one of the rocks suddenly looked excited and put down three letters; A-N-T at the end of my word 'fez' and when I looked at him strangely he told me that it was a type of bird!

To say that their young officer was somewhat embarrassed would be an understatement. As can be imagined the game soon came to a hasty end.

One of the funniest things I ever saw happened while I was stationed at RAF Valley in 1990. The *Red Arrows* flying display team were detached there while the markings on the runway at their parent unit, RAF Scampton, were re-painted. The technicians were working on an aircraft which was parked near the main hangar. It was a windy day and there were, as usual, lots of people visiting the station for various reasons.

All of a sudden, for a reason that was never determined, one of the aircraft dumped its bright red dye onto the ground. Taken up with the wind, everybody in the area was covered in the stuff. I attended the scene with another police corporal, Dave Roberts, soon after. We really had a terrible time trying to remain serious while dealing with irate contractors and upset airmen of various ranks, but the funniest of all was a group of cub scouts who were on a special visit! Everything, within about 200 meters was coated with bright red dye.

At first we were concerned about the possible health risks, but were quickly informed that it was harmless vegetable dye. That wasn't much comfort, however, to the scoutmaster, who had a group of very strange-looking pink cub scouts to get home! Their parents of course, would be just '*dyeing*' to see their kids and I could just imagine the look on the parents' faces when they met them from the bus.

No doubt they would see red!

drawn by 'Milne'

SKINNY DIPPING

Stewart McArdle

Corporal Stewart McArdle was part of the RAF Police Dog Demonstration Team in the early 1960s and recalls that the team were doing a series of demonstrations during a heat-wave.

Fortunately, they were staying at an RAF camp which had a swimming pool, so Sergeant Ken Hart, the man in charge of the team, approached the Gym staff to see if his men could use the pool to cool off.

While the staff had no objections, there was only one slight problem and that was that no-one on the team had brought swimming trunks with them. Again, the Gym staff said it presented no problem for them just as long as everyone was clear of the pool by 10am because the wives club had booked the pool at 10.30am.

That gave the team an hour or so to unwind. Subsequently, the all-male team, as naked as new born babes, wasted no time in getting into the cooling waters. All was going well and the guys were having great fun when suddenly the doors to the pool burst open and a group of ladies walked in, chatting amongst themselves. It only took a few seconds, however, for them to register that the men in the pool were all naked and the reaction of the women was simply to scream, albeit, that most of them were screaming with glee when they saw the bronzed athletic naked bodies before them.

It was only 09.45am and the guys often wondered whether their exposure was an honest mix up in timing by the Gym staff or whether they were simply getting one up on the *Snowdrops?*

Whatever the reason, it was certainly one performance by the RAF Police Dog demonstration Team that the ladies at that particular camp wouldn't forget in a hurry!

drawn by Tony Paley

KEEPING AN EYE OUT

Bill Barrass

Corporal John Frazer was serving with the RAF Police Flight on the island of Gan in the Indian Ocean in December 1970.

John had a glass eye, the result of a traffic accident some years before, and when he was sleeping, after completing a night shift, his good eye would be fast asleep but his glass eye was often very wide awake.

A native boy, Abdullah 'Waheed' Manikfan, was employed by the corporals to clean and do their laundry; he had a marvellous grasp of English, though unfortunately mostly swear-words and obscene phrases. (Initially, unaware of western-style laundry methods, Waheed would often wash the corporal's uniforms with *Vim* powdered bleach, with the result, not surprisingly, that they soon rotted to pieces.)

Waheed was fascinated by John's glass eye and occasionally John would leave a spare glass eye on his bedside locker while Waheed was working in the room. John would then leave the room but secretly watch Waheed at work from elsewhere.

Later, when he returned to the room, he was able to relate everything that Waheed had done while he had been away.

As a result Waheed became convinced that the glass eye lying on the bedside locker had magical powers and was always watching him.

drawn by Derek Knight-Messenger

BANK RUNS

Pip Waller

Corporal Waller and his dog Tarzan where stationed at RAF Finningley in 1961, where it was a regular occurrence for the RAF Police to be called upon to act as escorts for the unit accounts officer when he made his weekly trip out to the bank in Doncaster to collect the unit's payroll.

On this particular occasion Corporal Waller and his dog were detailed to assist and, because they were going into town, Tarzan was given a good grooming and Corporal Waller put on his best uniform. Before they left the unit, the accounts officer, briefed the driver and the escorts on the nature of the duty, the security implications should they be attacked and that, being out in the public eye, they were to remain smart and professional at all times. Shortly afterwards, they boarded the vehicles and set off for Doncaster. As they drew up outside the bank, the accounts officer and the escorts carried out a visual check to ensure that there was no threat lurking and, once satisfied, they left the vehicle and assembled on the pavement.

At that point, the accounts officer carefully checked his cap and tie and quickly brushed down his uniform with his hand before giving the order to enter the bank. Corporal Waller had been briefed to lead the way with his dog and as he did so the rest followed closely behind. It was just as they were entering the bank that poor old Tarzan had a desperate need to evacuate his bowels, which he did, on the large mat at the entrance.

Unfortunately, the accounts officer, whose attention was no doubt elsewhere, failed to notice this in time and promptly walked into the mess.

The smell inside the bank, the confusion at the entrance and the embarrassment of the accounts officer said it all.

Needless to say, Corporal Waller and Air dog Tarzan were never detailed for the 'bank run' ever again.

"...tell you, Adj, this station's going to the dogs."

drawn by 'Clayton'

NOT-SO-SALTY DOGS

Terry Langford

In 1952, the naval shore establishment at *HMS Grange Fort*, in Gosport had a small number of RAF personnel working on the unit, two of whom were RAF Police dog handlers. One of them, Corporal Terry Langford was a National Serviceman and the unit on which he served was close to his home and considered something of a cushy posting.

All was well in the world until a naval lieutenant commander approached Terry one day and told him that he had arranged for some senior naval officers to view a demonstration of what RAF Police dogs could do.

The officer was convinced that the deployment of dogs was useful in maintaining security and acting as a deterrent to thieves and anyone else intent on mischief. He was of the opinion that the Royal Navy should have its own patrol dogs and the planned demonstration was apparently his first step in convincing his superiors that dogs were an efficient and cost-effective way of providing that service. As such, he instructed Terry to attend with his colleague and their dogs the following day at 1400 hours where they would give the high-ranking visitors a demonstration of tracking.

While it all seemed a good idea, Terry attempted to point out to the officer that these dogs were not trackers but patrol dogs, trained to pick up the scent of an intruder in the wind. He further attempted to advise the officer that if he spoke to the commanding officer at the RAF Police Dog Training School and explained what he wanted then they would probably send down a fully trained handler and tracker dog to carry out the demonstration. His well intentioned advice however, was not what the ambitious naval officer wanted to hear and Terry was curtly informed to be ready for the demonstration as ordered.

The following afternoon a large number of very senior naval officers were assembled in an area where they could watch the demonstration close-up and shortly after, the two dog handlers brought their dogs out. At that point a motorcyclist duly arrived, towing a dummy, and set off into the distance, dragging the dummy behind him. The senior officers looked on with great interest.

After a suitable delay, to allow the dust to settle, the order was given to begin tracking. Terry set off first, in the direction that the motorcycle had taken, pulling his dog, who thought it was playtime. No matter what Terry tried to do, he could not get the dog to do something it had not been trained for; it was a disaster. The other dog handler was given the same instruction, resulting, of course, in the same farcical outcome.

The lieutenant commander was not a happy man, as all eyes turned towards him, but he could do nothing to turn the situation around. The senior officers, far from being impressed, started to drift away, muttering about the demonstration being a complete waste of their time, while the extremely embarrassed lieutenant commander tried desperately to retrieve something of his professional reputation that was fast disappearing.

Years later, Terry firmly believes that the disastrous demonstration that afternoon was probably the decisive factor that put the Royal Navy off establishing its own patrol dog section.

As for the ambitious lieutenant commander, Terry has no idea if he was ever promoted ... or simply keel-hauled!

A MINI DISASTER

Stewart Mcardle

I was on duty in the guardroom one day at RAF Machrihanish when the Boss shouted through from his office that he wanted a lift over to the other side of the airfield.

Before we could answer, *Corporal Sycophant* jumped up and promptly volunteered to take him. At that point, I asked *Corporal Sycophant* if he had ever driven a Mini before, to which he replied that he had. The Mini was parked facing the Bosses' office which was a pre-fabricated extension to the guardroom.

The boss jumped into the passenger seat and *Corporal Sycophant* got into the driver's seat.

Those of you who drove the Mini in the early 70s will remember how easy it was to select 1st gear but get reverse instead and *vice-versa*.

Yes, you've guessed it, *Corporal Sycophant* put the car in gear, put his arm around the back of the Bosses' seat, looked back, let the clutch out ... and promptly ploughed into the bosses' office, right through the pre-fabricated wall.

As you can well imagine, poor old *Corporal Sycophant* got little sympathy from the rest of the shift that day.

drawn by Richard Seal

OOPS!

Mike Nelson-Judd

It was a beautiful sunny Sunday morning in Bahrain sometime in 1963 and I was on duty at the barrier leading onto the airfield when the Station Commander drove up in his official car and slowed down. I dutifully put all my weight on the counter-balance, raised the barrier and smartly saluted.

However, instead of proceeding the Station Commander stopped halfway through to ask about the welfare of my family.

Unfortunately, at that point, the barrier which had been very well behaved up until then, decided to come down of its own accord.

Somewhat embarrassed, I quickly removed the heavy metal pole from the caved-in roof of his Vanguard and smartly saluted again; after all, it seemed the right thing to do!

Much to my surprise, the Station Commander drove away without saying another word.

I never heard another thing about it.

Now after forty-odd years, the whole world knows about it!

I WAS BUSY MUSING ...

drawn by Derek Knight-Messenger

ASK A STUPID QUESTION...

Author Unknown

Corporal *Snowdrop* was on duty at the main gate to an RAF base in West Germany one evening. A Summer Ball for the three services was about to begin in the Officers' Mess when a Naval staff car pulled up at the barrier containing a middle ranking Naval officer. Corporal *Snowdrop* asks to see the officers' identity card and the officer obligingly produces it.

"Thank you Sir," says Corporal *Snowdrop* but as he is about to raise the barrier to let the car in, the officer shouts out.

"Corporal, don't you entertain Naval officers in the Royal Air Force?"

"Of course we do Sir," replied Corporal *Snowdrop*, and promptly began to dance and sing, "*Give me the moonlight... Give me the girls...*"

On another occasion, Corporal *Snowdrop* was on duty one night in the guardroom when a young brash officer, who had obviously had one too many at the Officers' Mess bar, approached the enquiry window and called out:

"Corporal, call me a taxi will you,"

To which Corporal *Snowdrop* promptly replied.

"OK Sir, so you're a taxi."

drawn by 'APH'

UNDERCOVER CAPERS

John Law

The RAF wanted to give high security clearance to a senior NCO who was employed on a base in the south-west of the country. As part of the vetting process various background checks were initiated and enquires conducted in order to establish if the man concerned was *'squeaky-clean'* and that he had no *'skeletons in the closet'* that might represent a security risk by exposing him to possible blackmail to hand over secret information. (This all happened in the days when homosexual activities within HM Forces were not tolerated and as the enquiries progressed, suspicion that the man might be homosexual began to emerge and so the RAF Police were asked to conduct discreet enquiries.)

At the time, John Law was serving with the Special Investigation Branch (SIB) that covered the south-west area and was part of the surveillance operation mounted on the suspect that centred mainly around the man's flat and a gay club situated in the area of Derby Road in Southampton.

Covert observations may well be portrayed as exciting in the movies, but in reality they are mostly boring affairs, broken only by sudden and short periods of activity. John remembers well that during this particular operation a number of things occurred that helped to break up the monotony.

As always, the team *dressed down* to blend into the crowd and John was particularly talented in the area of disguise. After a day or two, the squadron leader in charge of SIB, no doubt bored with the inside of his office, decided that he needed some excitement and so headed south-west to visit the team. During a hasty lunch at a nearby pub he managed to consume a couple of pints of the landlord's finest brew before joining John and his partner, Rob Miller, in their car, which was parked around the corner from the suspect's flat.

Within the hour however, the beer he had consumed was beginning to make him feel uncomfortable and he desperately needed to pee. Being somewhat unprepared for sitting in a car for hours on end during observations, he asked John if he could use his *pee bottle* but both John and Rob declined to share their improvised urinals. On the point of bursting, the squadron leader frantically looked around in the litter on the floor of the car and picked up a small paper cup which he thought would do the trick, providing he controlled his flow and emptied the cup out into the gutter as it became full.

After adopting a suitable position in the back seat he successfully filled the cup and was just in the process of opening the door to dispose of the contents when the radio suddenly sparked into life with the message, *'Off, off, off!'*, indicating that their suspect was on the move.

John swears that it wasn't done on purpose, but as Rob rapidly accelerated away from the kerb, the contents of cup went all over the squadron leader and the back seat of the car. Realising, after an hour or so, that he had had more than enough excitement for one day, a rather damp and smelly squadron leader headed back to the safety of his office, leaving the *professionals* to get on with it.

Ironically, later that same evening, John and Rob were again parked up close to the suspects flat eating a curry in the car when again the call, *'Off, off, off!'* came over the air. Rob quickly hurled the remains of his meal out of the car window and started the engine. John, who was a much slower eater, had the same reflex action but unfortunately, his window was not open and the contents of the plastic tray were slowing running down the glass as the car moved off to join the others.

After a long day you can only begin to imagine just how untidy and smelly the inside of the car was. The following morning John did try and suggest to the others that it would be a good idea to rotate the cars, but for some reason they would have none of it.

After a few days of learning the suspect's routine John decided that they needed an *inside man* in the gay club and so *Taff* the youngest member of the team was selected. John of course, being the master of disguises, thought that Taff would look the part if he had an earring. Poor Taff still thought that it was all a joke until the young lady in the nearby Debenham's department store clipped the ring into his ear.

At the conclusion of the operation, John needed to phone his warrant officer and so he naturally walked into the local RAF Recruiting Office to make use of their facilities.

A very smart WRAF corporal suspiciously looked him up and down as he entered and when he placed his police warrant card on the counter she screamed for her boss crying, "Sir, there's a tramp in here who thinks he's a flight sergeant."

Indeed, John's disguise was so good that he had even been thrown out of a local *greasy spoon* café because he had failed to measure up to their rather undemanding dress code.

drawn by Richard Seal

drawn by Max Tate

RIDING SHOTGUN

Mel Price

Whereas in the Army the officers send their men to war, in the RAF the reverse is often the rule with the airmen sending the officers off to war in their *kites*! All too frequently however, RAF ground troops have had the opportunity of distinguishing themselves on duty at the *front-line*.

In the mid 1960s, as the security situation in Aden rapidly broke down, the RAF Police dog handlers had to travel through the notorious *Malla Straight*, otherwise known as *murder mile*, to get to the dog section to collect their dogs prior to beginning duty at the various military sites within the colony.

Travelling in a Bedford three-ton truck, one of the handlers would act as the armed escort for the RAF driver and as such would travel in the cab of the vehicle. As the cab roof was fitted with a hatch it was normal for the escorts to stand up on the seat with their head and shoulders poking through the hatch aiming their trusty Sten gun at whatever presented a threat to the free passage of the truck. The other handlers, equally armed, would be travelling in the back of the truck, ready to respond if required.

Well, they say there is always one for every situation and this was no exception! At the time there was one particular handler who fancied himself as *Sylvester Stallone* and always insisted on standing up in the cab, ready to take on the enemy, come what may. Unfortunately, a loaded Sten gun had a reputation of being rather unstable if the safety catch was off and the butt was banged down on any hard surface and great care needed to be taken to avoid a negligent discharge.

On the day concerned, there had been a threat issued of a terrorist attack and as such, everyone, including the ongoing shift of dog handlers, were just a little agitated. As they boarded the truck to go to the dog section *Corporal Stallone* quickly took up his position in the cab and, as usual, instead of holding the weapon properly and aiming it at any potential threat, he held it with the butt on the roof of the cab and the barrel pointing up into the air.

Apparently, *Corporal Stallone* thought it looked cooler that way and it allowed him to pose and wave to the service wives as the truck passed them by.

As they approached the *Malla Straight* the truck was going pretty fast and much to *Corporal Stallone's* surprise, as it went over a pothole in the road, the butt of the Sten gun was jarred and several rounds were fired into the air.

It was only by a pure stroke of luck that the discharge of his weapon did not invoke the Army sentries, posted around the nearby military married quarters, to return fire.

After that episode however, a lesson had been learned and *Corporal Stallone* didn't seem quite as eager to take up the posing position again.

"ON A 252, CLOT!"

drawn by 'Lemmon'

DIVINE INTERVENTION

Gus McGowen

Gan, being a small island in the middle of the Indian Ocean meant that everyone got around on bicycles; no matter who they belonged too! If you wanted to go to the other end of the island you simply took the nearest bicycle and someone else would eventually bring it back.

On one occasion in 1970 Gus recalls that the Roman Catholic padre had lost his bicycle and try as he might he could not find it anywhere. Now the good padre was also fond of a little nip now and again (as everyone else on the island was) and the RAF Police were well known for their BBQ's at the far end of the island in amongst the palm trees; more especially because they were the only section that could get such delicacies as crayfish and lobsters amongst other things.

So, after about three weeks of having to walk round the island the padre attended one of the BBQ's organised by the police and during the course of the evening Gus asked him if he had found his bicycle?

"No," he replied rather despondently.

Having consumed a few drinks by then, Gus respectfully reminded the padre that the Bible contained a saying about *'lifting up your eyes onto the Lord when in trouble'* and advised the padre to do the same.

Suddenly, a peaceful smile appeared on the padre's face and as he looked up towards the sky his eyes suddenly focused in on his bicycle hanging from a palm tree.

Gus recalls that the padre uttered a few of his own *sayings* that afternoon that were definitely not in the bible and many of them seemed to cast doubt on the integrity of the RAF Police!

"I'd like to see Chiefy's face when he sees this"

drawn by 'Canning'

SNOWDROPS IN THE SNOW

Derek McLeish, Neil Wilson & Gordon W Coull

The winters in West Germany were always harsh and the RAF Police who worked through the long dark nights strived as best they could to cope with the weather. However, when it snowed morale always seemed to improve.

With nothing much else to do, Corporal's Derek McLeish and 'Chuck' Dent were having great fun on one of the aircraft dispersal areas on a snowy Sunday morning, practising their hand-brake turns and anti-skid procedures in the virgin snow.

After a while, the two NCOs decided to park up and take a break and as they surveyed the dispersal before them they noticed that there was hardly a virgin patch of snow left.

After about five minutes or so, a mini appeared and drove up to the police vehicle. The squadron CO poked his head out and asked the two policemen to keep an eye out for the idiots who were messing up his dispersal area. Apparently, it made the work of clearing the snow and frozen slush much more difficult.

Both men assured him that they would give it priority!

The CO drove off, satisfied that the job was in capable hands – great times!

Neil Wilson recalls that the golden rule was that when it snowed unauthorised vehicles were not permitted to drive on the hard surfaces of the airfield until after the snow ploughs had done their job. He remembers one particular night shift at RAF Cranwell when a good three inches of snow fell in a very short time, transforming everything on the base into a winter wonderland. He was on patrol that night and responded to a report that a car was *wheel spinning* all over the place, including the airfield's taxi-way. Although he was unable to stop the car, he found it soon afterwards, parked in the Officer's Mess car park and a subsequent check revealed its owner to be a pilot. He duly recorded the details and prepared a report for his flight sergeant.

Shortly before going off-duty later that morning the wing commander in charge of airfield operations telephoned the flight sergeant to complain that the RAF Police had been driving all over his airfield during the night. The flight sergeant of course, took great delight in informing the irate officer that the culprit was, in fact, a pilot! The pilot concerned was later observed with a shovel in his hands clearing the snow from the pavements around the operations building.

Gordon Coull recalls that the winter was always fun especially when it snowed. The RAF Police out on patrol of the airfield always managed to build snowmen in various poses.

Sometimes, after a particular squadron had been working late, the ground crew driving back to the domestic site in their Land Rovers would take great delight in driving off the hard surface to demolish any snowmen that had been constructed by the police patrols or dog-handlers.

During one period of heavy snowfall that happened on numerous occasions and the squadron ground crew began to keep a tally of the snowmen destroyed. Soon after, a group of aircraft technicians going off duty in their Land Rover spotted a really well sculptured snowman in their sights and moved in for the kill... At optimum ramming speed the vehicle ploughed into the giant snowman and suddenly came to a crushing stop.

It seemed that some-one had come up with the bright idea of building the snowman over one of the many fire hydrants dotted around the aircraft dispersals. Although the snowman had been demolished, the Land Rover had suffered considerably and the poor ground crew, who had fallen victim to the ploy, were soaked to the skin in the freezing geyser which shot up from the damaged hydrant.

After that, snowmen, it seemed, became a protected species!

DOMESTIC VIOLENCE

Brian Burgess

It was a still, warm and humid tropical night at RAF Seletar. It was 1968 and I was sitting outside the main guardroom; eighteen years old and a long way from my mum!

"Come on Brian, let's go and have a look around *Seletar Hills*." It was Corporal Harry Wilson, a mature and married NCO who had taken me under his wing. We set off from the camp and Harry settled back into the passenger seat and pulled his cap over his face, placed his feet on the dashboard and asked me to wake him only in an emergency! We were out in one of our short-wheelbase Land Rovers, which, to facilitate the easy access and egress of the doggy men and their beasts, had no tailgate fitted.

An unhurried patrol around the large estate that contained many service *hirings* (rented accommodation for married personnel) was uneventful until I turned a corner and started to drive up towards a row of shops that also contained a small bar.

Suddenly, lying in the middle of the road, was a man being beaten quite violently by a woman with her handbag...

I gazed at the bizarre sight for a few moments and then the woman looked up, saw us, and ran off.

"Harry..."

"What?"

"Harry, there's a bloke in the middle of the road bruised and bleeding."

Harry, give him his due, quickly leapt from the vehicle and began checking to see if the unfortunate man was OK; he wasn't. Having ascertained that he was a serviceman I radioed back to Seletar to let the sick quarters know we were bringing in a customer. The poor bloke was very drunk and half unconscious and so we laid him on the floor in the back of the vehicle and I got in with him and sat on one of the bench seats, putting my legs over him and planting my feet against the facing seats for stability. Harry, driving, set off at a cracking pace and everything was going well until we came to the corner of a major junction which led to *Jalan Kayu* and the camp. Then two things happened almost at once: I held on for dear life as we careered around the bend and the bloke gently slid out of the back of the Land Rover, bounced once and then rolled into the large deep monsoon drain alongside the road.

"Harry…"

"What now?"

"The bloke just fell out the back."

"Oh shit!" Harry screeched to a halt, crunched the Land Rover into reverse and backed up the road towards the junction. We jumped out and found the poor bloke groaning in a heap at the bottom of the drain, now more battered and bruised than when we had first seen him. We quickly pulled him out and loaded him back into the vehicle but this time I positioned my feet firmly in place to ensure he didn't leave us again as we sped off towards the sick quarters.

Our casualty was duly received by the medics, who were totally unaware of what had befallen him. The Medical Officer asked how he came to be in such a battered condition and expressed great dismay at what domestic violence mixed with alcohol could do.

We said nothing but nodded in full agreement!

A WILD DOGFIGHT

Brian Burgess

With the threat of rabies always about in Singapore, a single bore shotgun was kept in the armoury in the guardroom at RAF Seletar, which was mainly used to despatch unwanted family pets that had been left behind, dangerous monkeys, and the wild dogs that roamed around in packs on the airfield.

On a particular nightshift one of the dog handlers telephoned the guardroom to report that he was trapped at the dog section after being surrounded by a pack of angry wild dogs that seemed intent on tearing him apart.

In charge of the shift that night was Flight Sergeant Barry Copp, who, besides being a real gentleman, was also my hero, mentor and Christmas dinner host. In short, he looked after me while my *knees were getting brown* and taught me the art of growing up in the RAF.

On hearing of the dog handler's predicament he instructed me to hand him the shotgun with some cartridges and ordered me to drive him to the dog section where he intended to despatch a few of those pesky dogs. On the way we called at the Airman's Mess, where we obtained some scraps from the duty cook. Once again, we were out in one of the short-wheelbase Land Rovers which had no tailgate fitted.

At the head of the approach road which led to the dog section the flight sergeant told me to stop and he promptly jumped out to have a quick *recce*. The pack of dogs however, numbering around ten, saw us arriving and immediately charged up the road towards us, much to the relief of the poor dog handler stuck in the office.

The flight sergeant quickly jumped into the back of the Land Rover and, with his back against the cab wall and feet spread out and planted firmly each side of where the tailgate would be, quickly loaded the shotgun.

"Drive Corporal Burgess!" he screamed, and we set off along the straight road with the ferocious pack close on our heels.

As the dogs charged along behind, the flight sergeant bunged out the scraps, which some of the dogs snatched up before resuming the chase. While the flight sergeant fired off a few shots, I concentrated on driving straight ahead and was not aware whether any of the wild, snarling beasts had been hit.

All was going well and I was really beginning to enjoy this diversion from the normal routine, until suddenly the Land Rover started to lose power. The flight sergeant also immediately noticed the loss of power as the dogs were obviously gaining on him with every bound.

"What the hell are you doing?" he shouted, with a voice bordering on hysteria.

Under extreme stress by then, I quickly scanned the instrument panel and to my horror realised that one of the dual fuel tanks was empty; I knew I had to physically change over tanks by turning the tap positioned under my seat. Acutely conscious that the vehicle was slowing down and that the ferocious pack was gaining on us, I frantically fumbled for the blasted tap.

The shotgun was a single-shot type so the flight sergeant was frantically reloading and screaming at me to speed up.

Suddenly, I found the tap, switched over and with a cough the engine came back to life and we abruptly accelerated away with my *rear gunner* blasting point blank at the remaining dogs, which were by then within snapping distance of his spread legs and the *family jewels*.

Eventually all the dogs were despatched and the dog handler rescued but I got a real roasting that night over ensuring that we always had sufficient fuel and my driving technique, but all in good spirit and with a wry smile from my hero, Flight Sergeant Barry Copp.

BARKING OUT ORDERS

Mel Price

At RAF North-Coates one day the Group Captain, being the station commander, decided that he wanted to have two RAF Police dog handlers with their dogs marching at the front of his parade when the Air-Officer-Commanding came to carry out his formal inspection of the unit.

Two handlers, one of whom was Corporal Mel Price, were chosen and ordered to attend the parade rehearsal. After sorting everyone out according to size, the station warrant officer, who was the parade commander, called the parade to *attention*.

At that point, the two handlers in unison yelled out 'STAY' and then swiftly came to attention.

The next word of command was to *turn left in column of route*.

Again, both handlers shouted 'HEEL', took one pace forward and did a left turn before coming to attention and then shouting 'SIT'.

The next word of command was *quick march*.

The parade started marching as the two handlers shouted 'HEEL' and then started off.

Although they were in step with each other, they were out of step with the rest of the parade marching behind them. The parade commander noticed the error and quickly bellowed out, the order, *'parade, change step!'* which the parade did, but so too did the two dog handlers, so the situation had not been rectified. Once again the order *'parade, change step'* was issued and the same thing happened.

Giggling started to be heard in the ranks.

The parade was quickly turning into a shambles as the parade commander bellowed *'parade halt!'*

The parade swiftly came to a halt as the two handlers shouted, 'SIT'.

As the parade burst into fits of laughter, the station warrant officer turned crimson with rage and the Group Captain was far from amused as he approached the handlers, demanding to know what the hell they were playing at.

It was Corporal Price who respectfully explained that as dog handlers they were always required to give the order to the dog before carrying out the action, which was precisely why Queen's Regulations recommended that dog handlers did not take part in normal parades.

The Group Captain was livid and demanded to know why no-one had told him. The mood of the station warrant officer was turning even darker as the Group Captain yelled at the two dog handlers to get off his parade ground.

Funnily enough, dog handlers were never detailed to go on a parade again. After the fiasco, whenever the station warrant officer set eyes on either dog handler his face was a picture, but there was nothing he could do about the day he lost the plot on the parade ground.

"Steady old dog, we must be brave"

drawn by 'Clayton'

DON'T FIDDLE

Norrie Pearce

At the end of 1969 I was a RAF Police dog handler stationed at RAF Scampton in Lincolnshire. In charge of our particular shift was Harry Rea, an acting corporal with nine years' service under his belt.

Now one could never describe Harry as the serious type and he couldn't wait for his discharge date to arrive. Consequently, he tended to cut every corner in the book and spent endless hours doing anything to alleviate the boredom of actually guarding the unit's bomber aircraft. One night, while on duty in the bomb dump, Harry came across a fire extinguisher at the entrance to one of the bomb silos, the type used to fight electrical fires. Bored as usual, he picked it up and started to practise his *cowboy* quick draw technique, aiming the extinguisher's pistol mechanism at his dog Bruce, a large, jet-black Alsatian.

While Bruce looked on curiously, Harry's fast-draw technique began to improve with time. All was going well until suddenly, as a result of all the practising, the seal on the pistol disintegrated and the extinguisher burst into life and rapidly emptied a great quantity of fine white powder all over Bruce, instantly turning the black dog into a pure white dog sporting a black nose.

It took some time afterwards to get the dog cleaned up, but again, it was a chore that helped Harry to pass off a few more hours on duty.

On another occasion, Harry and Bruce were patrolling one of the aircraft dispersal areas containing a number of huge Vulcan bombers. Bored as usual, Harry couldn't help but wonder what a particular button on the outside of the aircraft was for. Again, curiosity got the better of him, so he gave in and discovered to his horror that by pressing the button the entire load of *anti-Radar chaff* was instantly jettisoned onto the dispersal.

Seeking assistance, it took Harry and a few of his colleagues several hours to sweep up all the tin foil from the dispersal area, and a lot of explaining the following morning to the ground crew.

Harry later left the RAF and became Police Constable Rae of the Lincolnshire Police.

"The kit inspection due to take place at 0830 hours in cancelled"

drawn by 'Clayton'

A WHIFF OF SUCCESS

Mel Price

After coming out of the RAF, never wanting to take orders from anyone ever again, I started my own business making my own chemical products. Eventually my experience as a dog handler came in useful when I started to produce my own brand of dog shampoo and disinfectant. In developing the products I chose some of the best ingredients I could find as well as using expensive perfumes. My pride and joy however, was a lime scented disinfectant which had a beautiful fragrance. One day I happened to be attending a dog show and bumped into Terry MacHaffie, the RAF's chief training officer (dogs), who was showing his own dog that day. We got chatting at my stall and he ended up buying some of the lime disinfectant.

It was about three months later when he telephoned me to say how good the disinfectant was and placed an order for more. Shortly after, two five-litre containers were sent out to him. After another two months, he wanted some more, then a month after that, another lot was ordered; good business I thought. Later that year I was attending the RAF Police annual dog trials at RAF Newton when I got chatting to Terry again and during the conversation discovered that he owned very small dogs. Curious, I asked him how on earth he had managed to get through so much disinfectant in such a short time.

"Well," he replied. "It has such a beautiful fragrance that I put two cupfuls in my bath water every night, it makes me smell very nice." As I walked away, slightly bemused, I forgot to enquire whether he actually used any of the disinfectant on his dogs.

drawn by Richard Seal

NICE ENOUGH TO EAT

Stewart McArdle

In 1973 I was stationed at RAF Machrihanish on the west coast of Scotland. I recall that we dog handlers were preparing for the annual UK RAF Police Dog Efficiency Competition that year, which included a new test known as the 'Food Refusal'.

The new test involved placing a semi-circle of food in front of the dog, which was then recalled to his handler without touching the food; well that was the idea anyway!

At the time, we had a very good dog at the unit which had lots of potential, but no matter how hard we tried, we just couldn't get him to leave the food, and can after can of dog meat was gobbled up by the dog as he was recalled to join his handler.

In the end, I came up with the bright idea of making the food more repulsive to the dog, which I thought might at least be a start. I headed off to the cookhouse and, after explaining the problem with the chef, I managed to come away with a right assortment of curry powder, chilli powder, various types of pepper and anything else *anti-dog* that the chef thought might help.

The following day, we all assembled again to continue the training and, armed with my special magic mixture, I set about mixing it in with the dog meat. My mate then placed his dog in position behind the semi-circle of food and smartly walked away, ordering his dog to 'stay'.

We all watched with great interest as he then called his dog towards him. The dog moved forward, sniffed at the food, hesitated for a few seconds and then promptly gobbled the lot up before bounding over to join his handler.

Clearly the dog was into the more exotic types of cuisine and it was obvious that *Plan A* was a definite non-starter.

Unfortunately, while the dog enjoyed the food, the food didn't quite agree with the dog and for almost twenty-hour hours afterwards it couldn't stop farting – and boy did that dog produce one hell of a stink!

Eventually, however, with perseverance and kindness, we managed, in the end, to get the dog to leave the food when called back to his handler.

...On the other hand, the dog may simply have realised that rich food didn't agree with him!

Artist unknown

PLAYING GOOSEBERRY

Graham Aspinall

In 1987 I was a deputy RAF Police shift commander at RAF Waddington, where we police had just given up the job of checking to ensure that the large number of filing cabinets, cupboards and safes containing security material, that were dotted around the unit, were locked and secure, this task having been taken over by airmen/women detailed for guard duty.

Anyway, one dark winter's night a young, rather attractive WRAF, who worked in the telephone exchange, was detailed to carry out the check of the security containers. Because she was so scared of the dark, she came over to the RAF Police office to ask us to show her where the containers were located. A young acting corporal, no doubt trying to make an impression on her, quickly volunteered to show her around and the pair left the building.

A short time later, I was leaving the police office when I noticed the young corporal's Land Rover parked outside the Station Headquarters, unattended and with the engine running.

It was too good an opportunity to miss, so I quickly ran across to the vehicle and hid myself in the back, having first removed the ignition keys. Seconds later, the corporal and the WRAF came out of the building and got into the cab of the vehicle, not realising that the engine was no longer running.

It was only when the corporal tried to restart the engine that he noticed the keys were missing. At that point, while trying to suppress my giggles, they both got out of the vehicle again and quickly checked their pockets. When the keys were not found they both went back into the building, where apparently they searched every room, but to no avail.

In their absence, however, I replaced the keys in the ignition. When they came back out, the corporal got into the driver's seat while the WRAF went across to get a torch from the guardroom. While she was gone, the corporal's hand touched the keys and, although surprised, he said nothing.

When the WRAF returned with the torch the corporal announced that he had found the keys on the floor and soon after, the engine was started and they resumed the journey, with the young corporal still trying hard to impress the WRAF by driving like a maniac around the unit.

At one point, she remarked, *"You'll be the death of me,"* and that was my cue to pounce.

I popped up between them and said, *"And you'll be the death of me as well"*.

The WRAF gave out the loudest scream I've ever heard but his was a slightly delayed reaction; a loud *"Aaaaaaarrgh"*, followed by him taking both hands off the wheel and flinging them up in the air.

I've never laughed so much; the incident happened at about 2130 hours and I was still laughing at 0800 hours the following morning when we went off shift.

'OF COURSE IN MY DAY WE DIDN'T MIX DOGS AND BITCHES'

drawn by Tony Paley

A VIP VISIT

Taff (the dog) Jones

In 1931, at the age of 21, Douglas Bader was the golden boy of the RAF, excelling in everything he did; he represented the RAF in aerobatics displays, played rugby for the Harlequins and was tipped to be the next England fly half. But one afternoon in December all his ambitions came to an abrupt end when he crashed his plane doing a particularly difficult aerobatic trick. His injuries were so serious that surgeons were forced to amputate both his legs to save his life. Bader did not fly again until the outbreak of World War II, when his undoubted skill in the air was enough to convince a desperate air force to give him his own squadron. The rest, as they say, is the stuff of legend.

Flying Hurricanes in the Battle of Britain he led his squadron to kill after kill, keeping them all going with his unstoppable banter. Shot down in occupied France, his German captors had to confiscate his tin legs in order to stop him trying to escape. Bader faced it all, disability, leadership and capture, with the same charm, charisma and determination that was an inspiration to all around him.

In the early 1960s Corporal Taff (the dog) Jones was on his basic dog handling course at RAF Debden. It was a boiling hot day and the trainees were out on the grooming range, busy preparing their dogs for a very important visitor. Soon afterwards the VIP came into view and the course instructor, Ken Phillipson, quickly instructed the trainees to get the dogs off the grooming chains, ready to march smartly away in an effort to demonstrate just how busy the school was.

At that point, however, Taff's dog, Sheba, was getting quite agitated as she saw the VIP getting closer and in the confusion Taff forgot to attach the lead to her chain collar before unclipping the kennel chain. With sweaty hands almost losing their grip on the dog's chain, Ken Phillipson, who quickly realised what was happening, began to mildly panic as he ordered Taff to get his dog clipped on.

"It's alright Ken," Taff gleefully replied. "She's a leg-biter."

The VIP, of course, was none other than Group Captain Douglas Bader DSO RAF (Rtd)!

"He says if he's got to broadcast he might as well do it properly."

drawn by 'Clayton'

RAF POLICE RADIO PROTOCOL

By Chris Hill

Location - RAF St Mawgan in Cornwall in 1991. A transcript from a real RAF Police radio transmission between the Flight Sergeant in charge of 'D' Shift in the Police Control Room and one of his men out on patrol:

'Police Control, to Call-sign 43, message over.'

'Police Control this is Call-sign 43, send your message over.'

'Police Control, to Call-sign 43, if you have a radio with you, can you turn it on, over.'

A COLOURFUL SHIFT

Taff Jones

Mobile police patrolling the vast airbase at RAF Waddington in Lincoln were assigned colours as their radio call-signs. On one occasion, the following radio transmission was recorded:

'Amber Control, this is Pink, message over'.

'Amber Control to last call-sign, say again, over.'

'Amber Control, this is Pink, message over.'

Amber Control to last call-sign, identify yourself properly. We don't have a Pink call-sign, over.'

Amber Control, 'this is Pink, we do now, Red has just crashed into White, over.'

An Artist Goes to the Dogs (3) " ... *don't just play with the dogs.*"

drawn by Derek Knight-Messenger

MORE RAF POLICE RADIO CONVERSATIONS

John Moore

Location: RAF Bruggen in Germany:
'Control to Mobile Call-sign, message over.'
'Control this is Mobile Call-sign, send you message over.'
Control to Mobile Call-sign, Can you check out Area 7
Woods for evidence of an intruder? Over.'
'Control this is Mobile Call-sign, Wilco, over.'
'Control to Mobile Call-sign (on arrival at Area 7) – I can hear
FOOTPRINTS in the woods, over.'

Location: RAF Laarbruch in Germany.
Conversation between driver and passenger in Land Rover:
Passenger to newly arrived RAF Police Corporal driver.
"Where did you learn to drive like this?"
Driver – "I used to drive a tractor on my dads farm?
Passenger – Well this is not a farm, this is known as the
'bondu' so just take it easy.
Driver – "No problem."
Passenger – "Look out!!!"
Driver using radio – "Police Control this is Mobile Call-sign
22 – We have a slight problem with the Land Rover, it's stuck
between two trees and we can't get the doors open to get out,
over."

"Short back and sides and a bit off the tail."

drawn by 'Clayton'

SEARCH DOG ANTICS

Stewart McArdle

At the start of a *Search dog course*, in 1976, Stu Robinson was teamed up with a yellow Labrador named *Prince* who was a character in his own right. One day while the pair were out walking *Prince* suddenly took-off to chase a train, of all things. Later, the training school received a telephone call from the Railway authorities asking for some-one to go and collect the Labrador, which would not let the train leave the station!

Later during the course, Stu and his dog were conducting a search of a hangar and their progress was being videoed by the instructor, Dave Remnant, for training purposes.

After carrying out a free search, where the dog was allowed to run around the hangar to pick-up any lingering scent, the team went into a systematic search. *Prince,* however, kept indicating towards the metal plates which covered the heating ducts in the floor around the hangar, so Stu lifted one of the covers and *Prince* quickly disappeared down the hole and ran alongside the pipes, out of view.

Because Stu couldn't tell with any accuracy where his dog was, he lifted up another metal cover further on and looked down into the duct. As he did so, *Prince* appeared at the original duct, had a look around and quickly disappeared again.

Stu, who saw him, ran back to the original hole and called his dog who, promptly appeared at the second hole. Again, after popping up his head and looking around briefly, he disappeared again so Stu lifted a third cover and called out for *Prince,* who appeared again at the second hole.

The training exercise was swiftly turning into a farce and everyone watching began wetting themselves with laughter as the handler and dog tried to be at the right hole at the same time.

The exercise was called off and when everyone went back to the classroom to view the videotape everybody, except poor old Stu, were again falling about laughing at the antics of the dog and his handler.

On the same course Stewart McArdle had been teamed up with another Labrador called *Joe* and on this particular day he and *Joe* were carrying out a training search for hidden drugs in one of the Barrack blocks on the unit. After clearing all the rooms, the pair entered the toilets, which stank and where loud music was blaring out of one of the cubicles. The dog seemed more than interested in whatever was inside.

Stewart quickly looked under the cubicle door and saw a pair of Wellington boots with denim trousers draped round the ankles. He therefore issued a warning to the occupant that he was conducting a search and wanted him to vacate the toilets at once. The warning however, was met by total silence, other than the loud music.

Stewart quickly issued another warning and it too was ignored.

By then, Stewart was getting rather irate and after a third warning was ignored he kicked in the toilet door and was confronted by a transistor radio on top of the cistern and a set of empty denims draped over the toilet seat and the Wellington boots. He was livid, but before he could work out what had happened, Dave Remnant and a few of the other students came into the room roaring with laughter.

Joe, it seemed, had also contributed to the joke by farting as he entered the toilets, which provided the smell and added to the overall (*or denim*) effect!

Stewart of course, who always took his dog training very seriously, didn't at first see the funny side to it, until *Joe* indicated towards the transistor radio and a search revealed the drugs stashed inside! The moral; don't become distracted!

On another occasion, Stewart McArdle and *Joe* were carrying out a search for hidden drugs in another barrack block and had easily found three of the four items hidden within. The fourth, however, proved more of a challenge and so another careful systematic search was conducted.

After a while, *Joe* indicated towards a door and zeroed in on the keyhole. Stewart quickly bent down to have a look inside it and promptly got an eyeful of water.

Dave Remnant and his cronies were at the other side of the door with a syringe of water, just waiting for Stewart to take a peep into the keyhole.

drawn by Janner Pascoe

drawn by Richard Seal

BULLYING REPORT

Author Unknown

A recent report by the Equal Opportunities Audit Team (EOAT) has found that allegations of widespread bullying and brutality within the British Forces are, in the most part, unfounded. The EOAT, which travelled to every Defence establishment across the UK and abroad and interviewed staff from all three services, found surprisingly few cases of unfair treatment and bullying within the Army and Navy. When it came to the RAF, however, the report told a different story.

Complaints to the EOAT came from a total of 13,555 RAF members, compared with three from the Navy and one from the Army. While this statistic is alarming in its own right, it becomes horrific when one considers that each complaint represents a sad story of abuse, mistreatment and neglect.

As one senior RAF officer put it, "Each story is a sad indictment on the RAF. When taken as a whole, however, it demonstrates a reprehensible lack of regard for personnel on the part of RAF managers at all levels."

One young pilot from a transport squadron told of having to spend two nights in tented accommodation, despite the fact that there was an empty five-star hotel just 1km away. Another said that he had been forced to endure a gruelling fitness test every year since he joined in 1997. One airwoman alleged that she had been overlooked for promotion on numerous occasions, simply because she was fat, lazy and stupid. An aircraftman stated he had been refused permission to wear civilian attire to work, despite the fact that his uniform clashed with his eye colour. Another had been forced to wear uncomfortable safety boots for periods of up to eight hours straight.

An RAF clerk could not understand why she had been sent to work in a Joint military headquarters, "I have been forced to work for horrid Army people who just don't understand what the military is all about. I feel the RAF has victimised me by forcing me to do this... I will be seeking compensation."

Shockingly, RAF senior ranks are also subject to mistreatment. One SNCO stated, "I was deeply upset when I was addressed as 'Flight Sergeant' by an officer. He knew my name was Robert. It was just horrible – I have never been so humiliated in all my life."

A number of personnel complained of having to attend courses that were not relevant to their jobs, such as rigorous ground combat courses and drawn-out lectures on occupational health and safety. To add insult to injury, a young corporal was even ordered to pack up chairs in the classroom after one such course.

The huge backlash against treatment of RAF personnel should provide senior officers with a vital clue with regard to the massive retention problems experienced by the RAF in recent times. Over the past two years, the MoD has spent some £19.8 million looking into the issue.

Not all of the RAF's hierarchy, however, were upset by the revelations. Outgoing Chief of the Air Staff, Air Chief Marshal Sir E*** F***, KCB CBE DSO ADC BSc(Eng) FRAeS RAF, was quoted as saying, "I'm delighted with the result. I am very happy that our retention problems are due, in the most part, at least, to something as harmless as bullying. I thought everyone was leaving because of me."

PUBLIC RELATIONS

Stephen R Davies

In the summer of 1987 I was working with the RAF Town Show in Llandudno. I went there with Martin Carter and we took our Range Rover and a motorcycle along with us. The weather wasn't particularly good to us but nevertheless we certainly had some fun there and the kids loved both vehicles, especially when I came up with the idea of using the radio equipment to liven things up.

It was quite a simple idea really. While Martin supervised the kids on the bike, I was standing nearby but out of sight with a portable radio. Because the motorcycle radio was also switched on, I was able to talk to the kid who was sitting on the bike. As such, we would pretend that the bike was able to speak. I would start off by saying, 'Hello, I'm Norton, the talking police bike what's your name'? If for some reason, I wasn't able to hear the kid's reply, Martin would repeat it out loud and I would carry on the conversation. The kids, of course, thought it was great and it even fooled one or two of the parents.

The morning after coming up with the idea of the talking bike, the weather was rather dull and it had rained hard in the night. Now, although we were all out on the promenade bright and early, the public had decided, quite sensibly, to stay indoors. Anyway, a group of us were standing chatting to each other behind one of the caravans close to our motorcycle.

Suddenly, I noticed the rather straight-laced female squadron leader, who was in overall charge of the show, approaching. She hadn't spotted us and was no doubt wondering where everyone had got to.

I suddenly had an idea. As she drew up alongside the motorcycle, she bent slightly to examine it, whereupon the radio crackled into life with, "Hello, little girl, would you like to go for a ride in the country?"

Well, to say that she almost died on the spot would be a bit of an understatement. Of course, we all burst out laughing and from the look on her face I thought I had overstepped the mark. However, she actually saw the funny side of it and after that she wasn't quite so straight-laced.

To assist us at the show, we had a couple of trainee pilots who were supervising activities at the various mock aircraft. Being a pretty sociable pair, they quickly settled in with the team and seemed to possess a good sense of humour.

Now the unfortunate thing about public relations exercises is that they attract all sorts of unfortunate, if not somewhat weird, people. I must admit that they don't normally affect me too much but, for some reason, Llandudno seemed to have a couple of particularly classic and stubborn characters who liked hanging around our display. After a couple of hours I called them both over for a chat. I then indicated to one of the mock aircraft and suggested that they could be even more helpful over there, assisting the pilot who was on duty.

Within minutes they were making their way to the aircraft being supervised by Stuart. After a couple of hours I looked over to where Stuart was standing and, sure enough, he was being pestered by the two *characters* who, it seemed, were beginning to get to him.

In the meantime, I had organised a bit of a mini talent contest, using the public address system on our vehicle. Consequently, several pensioners, on holiday, were gathered around, having a good old sing-song. It was at that point that Stuart approached, not looking very happy. Apparently, one of his *'little helpers'* had told him who had sent them to him.

He set about protesting to me but I just picked up the microphone and quickly introduced him to the crowd as, 'Hunky Stuart the fighter pilot', who was going to sing us a song.

Well, being a pilot, he selected supersonic speed and was away back at his aircraft in no time at all.

As you can imagine, when the show finished, I had quite a reputation as something of a prankster.

Did you find this collection of stories amusing?

If you did then you may be pleased to know that we are planning to publish a sequel.

You can contribute to the collection by sending your stories and/or cartoons to Steve Davies at:

rafsp@woodfieldpublishing.co.uk

Thank you in anticipation!